FROM DIAGNOSIS TO TREATMENT

IN CHILD PSYCHIATRY

FROM DIAGNOSIS TO TREATMENT

IN CHILD PSYCHIATRY

formulated by
the committee on child psychiatry

Group for the
Advancement of
Psychiatry

Jason Aronson New York

This book includes two reports by the Committee on Child Psychiatry of the GAP: The Diagnostic Process in Child Psychiatry (Report No. 38) and From Diagnosis to Treatment (Report No. 87).

First Aronson Edition
Copyright © 1974, Jason Aronson, Inc.
Copyright © 1957, 1973
Group for the Advancement of Psychiatry
104 East 25th Street, New York, N.Y. 10010

FOREWORD

The most extraordinary thing about this volume is that the publishers, with admirable audacity, have brought together between the same covers GAP reports 38 and 87 separated by a span of sixteen years. A great deal of professional change has occurred in that time and one might have expected, with reason, that the two productions would have been ill-consorted and separated by an awkward generation gap. That this is not the case at all should not surprise us, since we have become accustomed to the fact that GAP reports, in general, do not seem to age with the rapidity of other psychiatric literature (alas). How this singular contemporaneousness is preserved with ever-changing committees and ever-changing assignments is the secret of GAP that is probably worth its weight in gold to any enterprising publisher. I am not sure, however, that the organization itself knows consciously how it brings this about. Committees, of course (and GAP is run on committees), are relatively ageless; committee members grow old and leave but committees continue so that the new and the old are constantly intermingled with successive transfusions.

There is also something very special about the Committee on Child Psychiatry even though others at GAP resist recognizing this. There is also the possibility—and this may still be another facet of the magic operating in GAP—that other committees are imbued with the same sense of specialness and of mission. Our committee, since I have known it over this decade, has dedicated itself to the task of those who work with children or are conscious of children, more conscious of childhood, and more conscious of their own function with regard to children.

Let me say something about the philosophy that has activated this particular committee and motivated its reports. The collective image of child psychiatry that emerges from the two reports shows a strong family likeness suggesting either that the second committee was trained by the first (which is not true) or that American child psychiatry has stabilized considerably in the last two decades. The commonalities are easy to discern. For both committees, the child is a "unique and distinct individual," and both believe that the study of ontogenetic change is essential to the understanding of the individual and that the family is the essential ambience of the developing child. The strong focus on "growth-promoting and growth-retarding forces" in Report 38 portrays the hand of Allen and is less explicit in the second report. As with American child psychiatry, the theory is predominantly drawn from psychoanalysis although not exclusively confined to it. It is the theory of the analytically oriented rather than of analysts and is therefore used more flexibly and less pedantically. One could refer to it as a dynamic eclecticism that permits a much wider coverage and consideration of etiological factors and is found in the more strictly Freudian approach.

The two committees share in a psychobiological concept of the child, in an appreciation of his mutual and complementary relationship with his parents, the role of certain universal anxieties conducing to symptoms, in the importance of constitutional differences existing from the beginning of life, and in the practice of assessing the child in terms of both his strength and his weakness. The humanism of the child psychiatrist winds through both reports, as well as the optimism of their outlook. This has been stated so succinctly in the preface to Report 87, that I cannot do better than to quote it:

> The discerning reader will no doubt notice that a spirit of optimism pervades the text in spite of many expressed doubts and concerns. This is characteristic of child psychiatrists in their daily practice. They are inclined to go about their work with much more hopefulness than the circumstances will often warrant. In large measure this is due to the fact that they are dealing with individuals during the plastic and changeable phases of the life cycle when the developmental forces often work hand in glove with the therapist. Child psychiatrists experience and expect more dramatic changes than their colleagues in adult psychiatry.

One detects here overtones from the favored younger child who has come to regard himself as special because, unlike his older brothers, he has retained the priceless contact with childhood through which all genius eventually gravitates.

One might have expected that the philosophy of outlook or the *Weltenschauung* would not change too radically within this period of time but it was surprising to find that many ideas deemed highly fashionable today were just as fashionable sixteen years ago, although perhaps under a different label. For example, in those olden days of the fifties, it was taken as axiomatic that parents changed as much as their offspring during development and that they could be more parentally proficient with regard to one developmental phase over another. They also took it for granted with less noise than we make today, that the reactions of parents may be secondary to primary problems in the child as much as the other way around and they were consequently less defensively defensive of parents. They were as clear as we are today that not only is symptomatic behavior often the best behavior available to the child under certain circumstances but that it would be less than healthy for him not to manifest it.

I have been speaking of the commonalities that have persisted in spite of the very changing world and have attributed this in part to the occult mechanisms of GAP and to the enduring qualities of the child psychiatrist. I would now add what I consider to be the major factor responsible for the impression of similarity that is given. The two reports both have a fundamental interest in process. Defined by Webster as "a continuing development involving many changes, steps or operations." Report 38 insists that "diagnosis in child psychiatry must be seen as a dynamic process" and Report 87 refers to treatment planning as "the process which takes place between the diagnostic formulation and the ultimate treatment recommendation." When one learns that the latest GAP Committee on Child Psychiatry is currently engaged on investigating the "treatment process," it becomes clear that the continued emphasis is not a matter of chance but basic to the approach. Child psychiatrists, throughout the United States, are taught their craft by the careful examination of process and in turn train others by the same method. It is through process that one finds out what is taking place in the child, between the child and his therapist, and in the therapist irrespective of the theoretical frame of reference, the treatment procedure for the diagnosis. Committeemen around a table, therefore may differ considerably in all these latter respects and yet respond with immediate understanding to the "process notes." As theory and technique may separate professionals, the consideration of process brings them together. It is for this reason that the process of treatment planning dovetails so easily with the diagnostic process, the classificatory process, and now the treatment process. It is surprising to me that with such a unifying principle at hand, comprehensive textbooks fail entirely to make more use of it and therefore remain uneven, theoretically confused, technically at variance and altogether incongrously put together.

The two reports share another characteristic found in most GAP publications: they are strongly motivated to stimulating the field and generating ideas in others. The committeemen often see themselves not as teachers and trainers but as sounding boards for past, present, and future developments. Report 38 states unequivocally that it is "not intended as a manual of procedures for the training of the personnel but rather represents the thinking and experience of this group of child psychiatrists regarding the importance of the diagnostic process," and Report 87 equally insists that it is "not intended as an end in itself but as a stimulus to further work in the same field." Since all these committeemen share an approach to the child and his environment that is developmental, dynamic, holistic, and representative of child psychiatric practice in the United States, they have every reason to believe in their ability to resonate to what is of most value to the field. It would not be an exaggerated claim to state that with this volume in hand (coupled with "psychopathological disorders in childhood"), one could join a clinic anywhere in this country and feel immediately at home professionally.

There is one final lesson that emerges from these "basic" books and this has to do not with how professions are taught but how one learns to be a good practitioner. There are undoubtedly some who read this volume for its rules of thumb, but the majority will understand the purpose of GAP as a sample collective knowledge dispassionately culled from "common sense and experience" and will become, as it were, members of the committee and therefore willing to bring their own "common sense and experience" to bear on the argument. They will regard the production not as a textbook but as a chunk of life offered by peers for consideration. The quotation from that good physician of the eighteenth century, Dr. Gregory, in the historical introduction to Report 87 was selected after very careful deliberation:

> . . . to cure the diseases of the Mind, there is required that intimate knowledge of the Human Heart, which must be drawn from life itself, and which books can never teach . . .

and when such knowledge is acquired, the successful application of it to practice depends in a considerable degree on powers which no extent of Understanding can confer.

In keeping with this wisdom, one can only reiterate that the fundamental purpose of this book is not to teach but to inform the heart.

E. JAMES ANTHONY, M.D.
The Blanche F. Ittleson Professor of Child Psychiatry
Washington University School of Medicine, St. Louis

CONTENTS

A. The Diagnostic Process in Child Psychiatry

B. From Diagnosis to Treatment in Child Psychiatry

THE DIAGNOSTIC PROCESS

IN CHILD PSYCHIATRY

I. INTRODUCTION

This report defines the nature and scope of the diagnostic study in child psychiatry and underscores its strategic importance in the care of emotionally disturbed children. Based on current clinical knowledge and on dynamic-genetic principles concerning normal and pathological child development, the report presents the diagnostic study as a comprehensive dynamic medical process. As in general medicine and in other medical specialties, diagnosis in child psychiatry takes into account the multiplicity of etiological factors which may be involved in the emotional disabilities of any one child.

The report describes the diagnostic procedures in clinical child psychiatry, outlines the collaborative work of the psychiatrist and other medical and non-medical specialists and defines their specific and unique contributions to the study and diagnostic formulation. It stresses the ultimate medical responsibility of the psychiatrist for the integration of the various clinical data into a working diagnostic evaluation and for the planning of comprehensive treatment in the light of realistic goals and a reasonably valid prognostic appraisal.

The Committee addresses this report to professional people who are considering the general problem of structuring psychiatric services for children. It is not intended as a manual of procedures for the training of personnel but rather represents the thinking and experience of this group* of child psychiatrists regarding the im-

*The membership of the Committee on Child Psychiatry during the period of the major work on this report consisted of the following:

Othilda Krug, Cincinnati, Chairman	Eveoleen Rexford, Boston
Frederick H. Allen, Philadelphia	J. Franklin Robinson, Wilkes-Barre
Anne R. Benjamin, Chicago	John A. Rose, Philadelphia
George E. Gardner, Boston	Mabel Ross, New York
J. Cotter Hirschberg, Topeka	Robert L. Stubblefield, Denver
William S. Langford, New York	Exie E. Welsch, New York

The Committee wishes to express its deep appreciation to Mrs. Ethel Ginsburg for her continuous active participation in the preparation of this report, especially for her contributions to the section on "History and Current Setting of the Presenting Problem" and for her valuable editorial assistance throughout the report.

The Committee is also grateful to Dr. Phyllis Blanchard for her help on "The Psychological Examination".

portance of the diagnostic process. The Committee hopes however that this report will be of value in psychiatric education.

While child psychiatry may be practiced in a variety of settings — private practice, inpatient and outpatient psychiatric facilities for children, or in clinical units in host agencies, such as courts, schools and foster care agencies or institutions — the nature and scope of the diagnostic process remain the same in all settings because they are determined by the nature of childhood itself. In this report the psychiatric clinic for children will be used as the setting to illustrate the areas and methods of investigation.

Comparison of adult and child psychiatry — The similiarities and differences between adult and child psychiatry are nowhere clearer than in the diagnostic process. The ultimate goals are the same: an understanding of the nature of the presenting problem and its etiology, and the development of a plan of treatment designed to eliminate, control or ameliorate the negative forces, while making the fullest possible use of the positive forces in the patient and his situation.

The areas of investigation are the same: the history of the presenting complaint including medical, social and psychological data which might throw light on the development of this problem, followed or accompanied by the study of the patient to learn as much as possible about the nature and severity of his illness and about biological, emotional and environmental factors which must be taken into consideration in planning for his treatment.

The broad outlines of the diagnostic process are the same: the collection, integration and evaluation of pertinent data; the identification of etiological factors, specific or multiple; and the formulation of a working diagnosis, prognosis and treatment plan.

There are other similarities: dynamic theories of personality development apply equally to child and adult; the selective use of psychological tests and other devices aid in differential diagnosis; the psychiatrist carries the medical responsibility for the consideration of organic disease and the final diagnostic and treatment responsibility based on his clinical judgment which is the end product of his training and experience.

However, there are some specific differences between child and adult psychiatry. The adult patient usually presents himself for consultation because of symptoms from which he seeks relief. With

4

the exception of the psychotic patient or the individual who is referred by an authoritative governmental agency such as the court, the adult turns to the physician voluntarily, albeit often reluctantly. The young child, on the other hand, seldom if ever seeks help actively. He is always brought to the psychiatrist by an adult who is responsible for his care, either because this adult is concerned about the child's health or adjustment or because such action has been recommended, urged or even ordered by persons or agencies in a position to do so.

The first approach to the child psychiatrist is usually made by the parents or by a referring source on behalf of the parents. The child patient may or may not accompany the parents on the first visit depending on the individual situation or the procedures established by the psychiatrist in private practice or by the clinic to which application is made. In an earlier Report, "Basic Concepts in Child Psychiatry" (GAP Report #12), this Committee discussed clinic intake policies and procedures as well as the impact on the parents of the need to seek psychiatric help.

Particularly in child psychiatry it is not enough to seek information about the parent-child relationship from direct observation of the patient alone. Diagnosis in child psychiatry is directed at an understanding of past and present interactions and at the strengths and weaknesses of the major persons in the child's constellation — the child, the parents or parent substitutes, siblings, other key relatives, and the personnel of schools and other social institutions who may influence his maturing personality.

The development of the psychiatric clinic for children as we know it today parallels the growing recognition of the interdependence of child and parents and the need to include the parents in the diagnostic study and treatment of the child. During the past quarter century these clinics have developed special staffing patterns and procedures to facilitate their work with the child and his family. The "clinic team" concept in child psychiatric clinics is a direct outgrowth of this experience. The child psychiatrist in private practice endeavors to include and involve the parents of his patients. In some instances psychiatrists in private practice are now duplicating the clinic team by making use of the services of clinical psychologists and psychiatric social workers.

Clinical classification is different for the child than for the adult;

the adult has lived longer; he presents more cumulative evidence of behavior patterns and structured defenses. Furthermore, clinical syndromes have been described more definitively for adults than for children. As a matter of fact, clearly delineated and universally accepted diagnostic classifications for children have not been established. In the words of one child psychiatrist, "We have yet to find a label that means what it says and says what it is."

The impact of organic disorder is potentially greater on the young child than on the adult. The disorder itself may be no more severe, but in the case of a young child it may produce sufficient anxiety either in him, his parents or both to affect adversely his subsequent physical and emotional development. The presence of organic defect is often less easily discernible in the young child, especially in infancy; in the adult's longer life span there will have been many more opportunities for the development and detection of chronic organic defect. The young child's attempts to compensate for defective vision, hearing or motor control may be viewed as willful misbehavior, while the basic organic defect goes unrecognized.

The adult psychiatrist sees the chronologically mature individual who, in contrast to the young child, can be said to be more nearly an end product of the major portion of the growth process. For the adult patient the diagnostic study and treatment goals are concerned with a personality structure already developed, although some modification continues throughout life. The child psychiatrist sees the chronologically immature individual who is in a fluid state of incomplete personality development, characterized normally by rapid physical and psychological changes. For the child patient the diagnostic study and treatment methods are directed toward helping him achieve sufficient freedom from obstacles to his growth so that he can move with reasonable security through succeeding developmental stages.

These are some of the differences between adult and child psychiatry; these and others will be discussed in more detail in the body of the report, first in the section concerned with basic assumptions and later in the section having to do with methodology — how diagnostic data are gathered, integrated and evaluated.

II. BASIC ASSUMPTIONS

In preparing this report the Committee agreed that certain basic assumptions are essential to the consideration of the diagnostic process in child psychiatry. These basic assumptions relate to current knowledge concerning the development of human personality.

The concept that a child's behavior reflects his attempts to adapt to a series of tension-producing situations is fundamental to the diagnostic study of children. The well-adjusted child's methods of adaptation are personally gratifying and socially appropriate. The emotionally disabled child's adaptive attempts are ineffectual and only partially satisfying, and they may be experienced internally as distressing symptoms. As outer signs of the disability they may be manifested in behavior which is socially unacceptable and often disturbing to others.

Diagnosis involves primarily an investigation of the child's relative successes and failures in mastering in orderly sequence certain universal anxieties which confront all children as they move through the several stages of personality development. In general, the major tasks in this growth are directed toward the achievement of a biologically satisfying utilization of life energies (the libidinal or psychosexual and the aggressive drives) through constructive patterns which are socially and ethically satisfactory.

The delineation of those specific areas which have been seriously impeded at a particular chronological age must be based on the body of knowledge concerning normal personality growth. It is a distinctive feature of child psychiatry that all findings are weighed against the developmental norms for the successive, changing stages of growth. Basic to this concept is the belief that normal personality patterns evolve out of interpersonal relationships. As a unique and distinct biological organism, the child is always interacting in varying degrees with external social forces, especially within the family in early years. In infancy he depends totally on his parents for the primary satisfactions of loving care and for the protection necessary to sustain life. These lay the foundation for his further biological and psychological maturation which in turn progressively stimulates the inherent and newly emerging energies that increasingly strive for satisfying expression. To meet these successive changing needs the child again depends on adults, first on his parents and later on others in his broadening society. As the unique aspect of childhood, the dependency relationships provide the framework through which the child is helped to develop an awareness of himself as an organized separate individual whose behavior patterns are consistent with both individual and group living.

The growth of the child's sense of his own identity as a unique and distinct individual is accomplished within the successive developmental phases through certain observable processes of differentiation. In the earliest months the infant is in a relatively undifferentiated state of oneness with his mother. But gradually as the child experiences minimal and hence tolerable frustrations of his basic needs and is satisfied repetitively by his mother, he more actively turns toward her with increasing confidence and patience. He learns that he is separate and different from his mother yet dependent on her and his environment. In the normal, mutually gratifying, symbiotic relationship with his mother the infant's and mother's needs are complementary, for in anticipating and meeting her child's needs the mothering-person is also fulfilling her own mothering function.

Intimately associated and concurrent with this process, the child's neuro-muscular, intellectual and emotional growth leads to an awareness of his bodily parts and their functional differentiation. He also becomes aware of his increasing needs and greater energies for pleasurable and rewarding muscular activities such as reaching, walking, talking and controlling elimination. He strives to master some of his bodily functions so that voluntarily and purposefully he can direct his own actions to satisfy some of his needs. This self-sufficiency is attained through certain appropriate prohibitions and prescriptions. From the parents the child needs some actual protective limitations along with their support and guidance in becoming aware of socially approved standards and in learning the skills and techniques required for gratifying and acceptable behavior. In a sense the outcome of infant development is the increasing ability to bear tension.

Continued physiological maturation and expanding social experiences within the family contribute additional qualities to the child's sense of his own identity. When he begins to recognize the relationships between his parents and siblings, his egocentricity and possessiveness yield to a more precise ego differentiation. He also modifies his previous self-image of narcissistic omnipotence when he is confronted by the unique and exclusive relationship between his mother and father, as he naturally at this stage directs toward them his first diffuse and early genital tensions and his curiosity about the differences between the sexes and between children and adults. To resolve the resultant conflicting feelings of love, anger, rivalry, guilt and fear inevitably created by these universal triangular life experiences, he again needs the guidance of others. He needs adult understanding; a kindly, firm, appropriate balance of limits and permissiveness; and sound parental standards for identification in order to attain a valid acceptance of himself, — of his own biological sex, of his actual native aptitudes, and of his realistic position with his parents, siblings, peers and teachers. The adaptive capacities of the parents help the child achieve this type of identity enabling him to take some initiative and responsibility for his own behavior. The child needs parents who, first individually and somewhat differently as man and woman, and then together as husband and wife, and later as father and mother, have attained the maturity of enjoying and sharing their mutual creative responsibilities in fostering his continued growth.

The diagnostic process, therefore, must include two essential areas of investigation, each with its special characteristics but each understood more fully in its reciprocal relationship with the other. These are (1) the child himself, his basic physical and intellectual endowment and the inner biological and psychological forces and behavior patterns or ego mechanisms which emerge in the development of his own individual identity, and (2) the environment and its social forces which influence the child as he matures. In the exploration of dynamic and genetic factors, any unilateral approach precludes acurate diagnosis. Both the child and his society must be understood separately and in their interactions. The recognition of this necessity for including the family in the diagnostic process has differentiated child psychiatry from *traditional* adult psychiatry. In contrast to the adult with a more structured ego, the child is

9

still developing as an individual and is not only more flexible but also more vulnerable to the environmental forces around him.

The diagnosis of child pathology requires first of all the accurate delineation of those aspects of development which are primarily disturbed together with some reasonable hypotheses concerning the multiple factors that might have operated to cause the deviation. To construct a psychodynamic formulation requires a frame of reference which is based on the assumptions derived from accumulated clinical data. One basic assumption is that behavioral disabilities arise in an interpersonal milieu in connection with experiences that evoke or reactivate within the child a feeling of helplessness or vulnerability felt as an anxiety. This anxiety may be provoked by either realistic or fantasied threatening situations or by the child's actual or contemplated counter-measures directed against those situations. Its intensity, which reflects the child's valid or distorted estimate of the potential destructiveness of the threatening experience, will depend partly on the nature and intensity of the external challenge or precipitating factor and partly on the child's adaptive capacity as determined by his particular personality structure. Certain common challenges are inevitably experienced during the course of the child's growth. The degree to which they become severe threats varies with the age of the child and with the level of psycho-socio-sexual maturity that he has reeached at any given chronological age. The usual challenges of life may be experienced as severe threats by the immature child with limited ability to tolerate stress, while exposure to extraordinary environmental stress may threaten even the relatively stable child.

The universal primary anxiety connected with loss of love and protection is intensified initially or reactivated later by actual or expected abandonment or deprivation. This might occur with any separation from the parents, such as hospitalization, or with punitive threats of desertion. The common anxiety associated with mutilation and disability may become overwhelmingly great if the child is physically assaulted or threatened with any bodily harm, such as accident, disease, or even the physical injury inherent in a simple tonsillectomy or other surgical procedures. He may also be more vulnerable to this anxiety if, burdened with illogical guilt, he anticipates retaliation for his own destructive impulses. The anxiety associated with his sense of defeat about his performance and his feeling of inferiority and disgrace about his adequacy as a person compared to his own and others' standards may also disrupt the child's adjustment. This is often true for the child who actually has some disability but it occurs also when a child imagines he is defective.

When the child fails to deal adequately with these external conflicts or environmentally-stimulated anxieties, the process of symptom formation is set in motion. He may resort to earlier behavior patterns which had once been successful in coping with previous developmental tasks. But at best this attempt is only temporarily effective. This process of symptom formation might be illustrated by excerpts from the case history of Jimmy, a greatly over-indulged child of 8, whose basic insecurity was intensified by the arrival of a new sibling. He reverted to the earlier pleasure of persistent thumb-sucking which had previously been relinquished at age 3. This method of coping with his reactivated infantile needs was incompatible with society's expectations of the older child as well as with his own internalized standards and wishes as a growing boy. Moreover, he developed anxiety and guilt over the forbidden hostility he felt in response to the environment which frustrated his infantile impulses. Jimmy first attempted to solve his various internal and external conflicts by compulsively and aggressively repeating the former self-satisfying activity, namely the thumb-sucking. But this method failed as an adequate compromise; it afforded only partial satisfaction for which his guilt, nevertheless, demanded the penalty of personal suffering, energy diffusion and social disharmony. His various tensions were reflected in marked irritability, distractibility, feelings of shame and inferiority, and social withdrawal. In Jimmy's case his continued internal conflicts as well as further parental disapproval led to another equally unsuccessful solution when, along with a diminution of the thumb-sucking, he developed a new combination of patterns manifested as a severe animal phobia. In the face of similar conflicts some children might develop anorexia or vomiting, or over-eating and biting, or demanding, possessive attitudes. In each case, the child has resorted to some compulsive repetitive pattern or to a composite unitary action derived from earlier mechanisms. Although these methods result in some dependency satisfaction through the parental inter-

11

est and care elicited by the disabilities, the child is distressed and maladjusted. The degree to which his energies are bound and depleted by these conflicts determines the extent to which he is blocked in his further growth.

The type of emotional or behavioral disability which results is determined by the specific configuration of ego mechanisms utilized by the particular child. It is manifested in physiological, psychological or conduct disturbances which are the clinical signs and symptoms of anxiety itself or of the child's attempts to allay the anxiety. In any case the symptom consciously or unconsciously selected is often related to specific areas of parental emotional disturbance. Although the behavioral pattern may be dissatisfying to the child and unsatisfactory to society, it does serve the child in reducing or avoiding some of his anxieties.

The child's pathological response to anxiety may represent varying degrees of ego-disintegration. He experiences the threats as a destruction of his internalized body images — either of the existence of the body as a whole, or of its internal or external organs, or of its continued functioning in an effective and acceptable manner. This breakdown of ego integration is a psychological regression and may be called a "de-differentiation", analogous to the more primitive physiological dysfunctioning in organic pathology. On both the physical and psychological levels, the organism reacts to stress with a defensive attack against the dangerous stimuli by reverting to some previously effective pattern as a starting-point for re-establishing its structure and healthy functioning. In physical healing the cellular response is helpful in attacking noxious agents and restoring the physical integrity. An analogy might be found in the response to psychological stress; earlier successful behavior patterns are reactivated as defense mechanisms for mastering anxiety and for re-integrating the appropriate functional capacity of the ego.

Diagnosis in child psychiatry must be seen as a dynamic process through which are evaluated all the growth-promoting and growth-retarding forces in the child's life as they interact to produce various conflicts and the particular modes of solving them. It is more than the classification of a child in a nosological system based on the clinical observation and description of the presenting signs and symptoms of deviant behavior. In a sense then, it consists of an

12

evaluation of the functioning of the child's ego, of his integrative capacity, strength and flexibility. It involves an assessment of the nature and intensity of specific anxieties including the time and setting of their onset. Child psychiatric diagnosis delineates the areas and degree of regression as well as those pathological defense mechanisms used in the regression .It identifies also the healthy ego mechanisms utilized in the past and present in adapting to the normal developmental tasks of ordinary experiences and to any unusual or critical life situations. It takes into account any unevenness in the different spheres of personality development. It encompasses the concept that the disability itself represents a strategic withdrawal to a partially regressed level for re-grouping or rallying the child's strengths and that this constructive aspect of the child's disability can be supported for his recovery. In this appraisal it is also important to weigh the ego functions against the nature and strength of the internal drives arising in the biological processes and to recognize that the effectiveness of the ego's defenses against anxiety and the efficiency of its executive mechanisms are largely determined by the intactness and healthy functioning of the total organism, especially the neuro-muscular system.

The comprehensive evaluation of the child's ego functioning takes into account the two-way nature of his relationship with society. The child himself plays an active part in the interaction with his parents and others. Certain constitutional factors may lower his inherent capacity for the effective utilization of positive life experiences. Even in infancy certain characteristics of the child, such as his motility pattern and degree of sensitivity may influence the maternal attitude. A young child's repetitive unrewarding responses to mothering efforts may foster tensions and lead to the vicious cycle of an uncomforted child and a frustrated mother trying desperately to be a good mother. On the other hand, this process may be set in motion by the mother who, in a distorted identification with her child, responds to him as a symbol of an unsettled past. Unhealthy parental attitudes arising from previous or current significant relationships or from social or cultural factors may be displaced to the child so that the parent does not realistically perceive him or his needs. The child thus threatened and deprived may react aggressively in his frustration; he may be forced to turn back to earlier self-satisfying activities. His behavioral responses

13

then reinforce the distorted identifications of the mother so that tensions increase, and neither mother nor child gains from their relationship the gratifications necessary for each. As an example, severe emotional disturbance in the mother may so distort her perception of early infantile needs that adequate normal symbiosis is never attained. Such children, when they do not die of inter-current disease, are likely to show primary atypical development or mental retardation. Their behavior may represent fragmented aspects of developmental stages which have never have been fully mastered or integrated into the personality.

Basic to the understanding of parent-child interactions is the recognition that the parental capacity to meet a child's needs may vary greatly in his different phases of growth. The child's normal behavior at one stage may elicit healthy parental responses whereas at another it may reactivate the parents' immaturities around old conflicts pertinent to that level of development. In defining parental attitudes such terms as "rejecting mother" or "competitive father" are as stultifying as is the diagnostic label of "conduct disorder". Dynamic diagnosis is dependent on an accurate determination of those specific developmental areas in which a parent may be "rejecting" or "competitive". For example, a mother may satisfy completely her child's needs for oral dependency only to fail seriously, because of her own anxieties, to meet his increasing need for greater self-expression. Similarly significant is the evaluation of whether a "competitive father" is rivalrous with the dependency of his young son or with the masculine strivings of his growing son. Inadequate parental responses to the child at any level may vary from over-indulgence and the excessive permissiveness of prolonged earlier satisfactions to the overly ambitious and premature stimulation of more grown-up behavior in anticipation of a later stage in development. For normal growth the child needs to exact the appropriate satisfactions to be derived from each stage of development in order to proceed to the next. At the same time the mature gratification of the parents in helping the child at each step serves as a foundation for a continuing mutually beneficial relationship. A major aim of the diagnostic process is the understanding of the breakdown or lack of development of this healthy interaction as it gives rise to behavioral disabilities.

The diagnostic study is a dynamic process which offers new

relationships and potentially meaningful experiences to the child and his parents as they are helped to face their problems together and to reveal the various biological, psychological and social factors involved. It is based on a sound knowledge of both normal and pathological development and function and on an awareness of the continuous interaction of all the psychobiological and psychosocial forces. This understanding demands a multi-facetted approach; no unilateral study can effectively reveal the cross currents and significant forces in a total family situation. Sufficient historical data about physical, psychological and social factors; an adequate evalution of the child's current levels of physical and psychological functionings; and valid appraisals of his native physical equipment and intellectual endowment are all necessary. Therefore, the psychiatric clinics for children are staffed and structured on the basic assumption that the diagnostic process is a collaborative process utilizing the specialized methods of several professional disciplines to investigate the various diagnostic areas. In addition, the psychiatric clinics and other child diagnostic facilities take into account that a special sensitivity to the meaning of the different diagnostic areas is essential in planning comprehensive studies and in insuring their final integration. The diagnostic process for children is therefore developed through the leadership and direction of the child psychiatrist whose specialized training provides the skill and experience for carrying the ultimate responsibility of synthesizing the various diagnostic data into a comprehensive diagnosis of the child in his environment.

The separate diagnostic areas, their particular investigative procedures and their specific contributions to the total diagnostic formulation are considered in further detail in the next section of this report.

15

III. THE DIAGNOSTIC PROCESS

A. History and Current Setting of the Presenting Problem

1. *Referral and Application* — The term "presenting complaint" as it is known and used in general medicine and in adult psychiatry is not pertinent to child psychiatry, since the "complaint" is not made by the patient but is usually registered by an adult to whom the child's behavior presents a "problem". It is, therefore, a "presenting problem" which is brought to the psychiatric clinic by an adult, usually a parent who may be sufficiently troubled to come on his own initiative or whose application is stimulated by another person or agency.

The most significant complaints of parents are those given initially and spontaneously, even though they may not always concur precisely with those suggested by the community resource which stimulated the application. In a school referral the chief concern is apt to be around the child's academic achievement or social adjustment; in a court referral the emphasis will be on symptomatic delinquent behavior; while in a referral from a medical resource the emphasis may be on more specific neurotic or psychotic symptomatology, psychosomatic disorders or developmental deviations. This may also be true if application is made directly by the referring source, which will naturally be concerned with its own area of specialization or jurisdiction — the social agency, the school, the court, the pediatrician or family physician.

Implicit in the intake process of a child psychiatric clinic is the development and maintenance of a good working relationship with referring sources. An understanding of the way in which the clinic referral is presented to the family and of the relationship of the referring source to the family facilitates the diagnostic study.

Regardless of the source or manner of the referral, the first area of investigation is the parental attitudes toward psychiatric help. The diagnostic process actually begins with the parents' decision, voluntary or forced, to seek psychiatric help for the child. A beginning understanding of parental attitudes can be achieved by learn-

ing whether parents are actually motivated primarily by their own concern about the child or by pressures from others in the community. This includes consideration of the parents' awareness of their own involvement in the problem: whether they feel excessive guilt and self-blame or project the total responsibility on the child, on some illogical physical cause, on the school or on other physicians.

Further insights are gained concerning the parents' feelings about the child and their own capacity to participate in the diagnostic study as one begins to understand their conscious and unconscious desires and expectations from psychiatric help. Apparent readiness may hide great resistance, which may be reflected in the child's degree of accessibility in the psychiatric examination. But whether the parents reveal feelings of anxiety, self-criticism and guilt, or complete irresponsibility or hostility either to the child, the referring source or the clinic, the goal of the psychiatric clinic is to provide understanding support to enable them to express the negative reactions which might otherwise block their participation in the diagnostic process.

Time and skill devoted to this initial exploration of the presenting problem enable the parents to take the steps which will involve them and their child in the diagnostic process. All expressions of feeling and observed attitudes are grist to the diagnostic mill. This is true for the parents' reaction to clinic procedures, as well as for the way in which they tell the child about the clinic or express concern about the impact of the clinic experience on the child. The possible variations on the theme are all facets of the parents' anxieties, of their sense of failure, their hidden or manifest hostility, and their fear of being revealed through the child, as well as their concern lest the child find in his relationship with another adult the satisfactions which they presumably were unable to provide. By helping the parents interpret the clinic experience to the child and by dealing with the parents' own anxieties and misconceptions, the clinic lays the groundwork for the kind of relationship on which comprehensive diagnosis depends.

2. *Developmental History* — The specific symptoms and presenting problems which the parents describe at intake serve as a point of departure for an inquiry into the child's longitudinal development. Some organization of historical data must be kept in mind, but formal history schedules, rigidly used, may actually limit the

scope and meaningfulness of the data. In a broad sense it can be said that everything that has happened to the child is of importance in understanding the nature and significance of the present problem. Certainly his feeling about what has happened to him and the feelings and attitudes of significant adults in his life are of major importance.

The sequence in which historical data emerge and in which associations to them arise provides valuable clues to the meaning of these events to parent and child. Factual data about the mother's pregnancy and delivery can lead naturally to some discussion and understanding of the mother's concept of herself as a woman and of her attitudes about her children. Age at weaning, dentition, walking, talking, development of motor skills, toilet training and similar specific facts may be ascertained easily since many parents have such data readily available. If they are not readily available, that fact is equally important. Certainly a consideration of habit patterns — eating, sleeping, elimination, masturbation, etc. — offer not only facts but often highly charged emotional material. The investigation of how various habit patterns were acquired and dealt with often reveals parental attitudes which were significant in the child's early emotional development. The original interactions with parents and siblings should be carefully explored, including any family disruptions such as severe marital discord, separations, the birth of siblings and illness or death of relatives. Information as to the age of the child when such events took place and how they were handled both by the child and those closest to him will aid in evaluating their influence on the child's psychosocial growth.

The child's level of development is another major area of concern. His physiological maturation, sexual development and social adjustment in relation to what is expected at a given age represent the framework within which a multi-dimensional picture of the child begins to take shape. However, his present level of development cannot be evaluated without historical data about the rate, sequence and consistency of his growth, such as any unevenness in the developmental history or in the child's adaptive capacity or sudden acceleration or regression and the attendant circumstances.

The child's medical history is of major importance and should be ascertained in every case. A psychodynamic evaluation and a thorough review of the child's past and present physical health

are not mutually exclusive; they are inseparable parts of a full understanding of the child. Of particular significance is the age or developmental phase at which illness occurred and its impact on the parent-child relationship and on the child's subsequent development. As important as the known episodes of childhood illness or accidents and their sequelae is the information which can be obtained from parents or other sources about undiagnosed fevers and marked changes in behavior which may have been associated with episodes of organic illness. In the course of getting a developmental history one may also find clues to defective vision, hearing or motor coordination which can be pursued in subsequent examinations of the child.

3. *Social Setting* — The importance of information regarding a child's school experience is clear. The school history will reflect the ability of the child to separate himself from his family and establish himself as an individual in a group of his peers under an authority other than that of his parents. Information as to his grade progress, subject achievement, scholastic behavior and attitudes will be available from the school. His intelligence and general ability may have been tested formally in the school setting, in which case that information should also be obtained. Knowledge of the child's interrelationships with his peers, his teachers and those in authority is essential to an understanding of his adjustment as an individual. As part of its responsibility to the child it is essential, of course, that the clinic know the school, its auspices, policies and general level of acceptance in the community in order to evaluate the individual child's adjustment to it.

The domestic setting of the child includes not only members of his immediate family but in some instances other relatives, household employees or others living in the home. They are not ordinarily interviewed directly but since each may play a significant role in the life of the child, it is useful to know something of their personality, health, educational level and general social adjustment, as well as their attitudes toward this child and toward the difficulties for which help is being sought.

The general cultural, ethnic and economic standards of the family are valid subjects of inquiry if one is to achieve understanding of the child and the setting in which he finds himself. While the parents' report on cultural, ethnic and economic standards may be

19

colored by their own status needs and relationships to their environment, this too is useful information which can ultimately be checked against the clinic's knowledge of the community and, in the older child, against the patient's activities in recreational, religious and other groups.

In a child psychiatric clinic, it is usually the psychiatric social worker who implements psychiatric policy at intake and in many of the clinics continuing relationships with referring agencies and other resources in the community. The initial work with parents to interpret the clinic's service, to obtain a developmental and social history, to collect other pertinent data, possibly through home or school visits as indicated, and to schedule the physical, psychiatric and psychological examinations of the child have traditionally been assigned as the psychiatric social worker's function in the diagnostic process. In many clinics today, the psychiatrist interviews the parents at some point during the diagnostic process. He may participate in getting the history, especially developmental and medical data, or in helping the parents learn how to prepare the child for his initial psychiatric visit and other examinations. More often he may be the staff member who interprets to the parents the clinic's findings and recommendations.

As the clinic's representative to referring sources and to parents at a point where they are particularly sensitive and vulnerable, the psychiatric social worker must exercise professional skill and judgment in making available the services of the clinic. The manner in which this is done will influence, either positively or negatively, the community's understanding and use of the clinic, and the parents' readiness to involve themselves and their child in the diagnostic and treatment process.

B. The Physical Examination

As a basic aspect of the diagnostic process, the appraisal of the physical reality of the child includes an evaluation of data both from the medical history and from the general physical examination and special studies. Although usually the physical studies have already been done when the child is referred for psychiatric diagnosis, the child psychiatrist must be concerned with the adequacy, interpretation and integration of these previous studies. He must decide whether further studies would be helpful or in some in-

20

stances even of crucial importance. This is especially true when physicians who over-emphasize emotional factors refer children without having carefully assessed the child's somatic status. When children are referred from non-medical sources, it is the responsibility of the child psychiatrist to plan for reliable physical examination. In clinics or in private practice child psychiatrists should have good working arrangements for obtaining adequate physical studies by competent physicians. Although it is ordinarily less desirable for the child psychiatrist himself to do the physical examination, he may do so prior to beginning psychotherapy with the child, provided he is competent and is comfortable in doing the examination. Much confusion is avoided for both the psychiatrist and the child if such an examination is done in the usual appropriately-equipped examining room, either within or outside the psychiatric facility, rather than in some makeshift setting. However, regardless of the setting or the examiner, adequate physical evaluations are an integral part of the clinical practice of child psychiatry.

Certain information about the child's past and present medical status, including developmental sequences, is required in order to understand the impact that physical factors have had on his personality and on the presenting problem. It is important to assay the effect upon the child of any previous physical procedures or hospital experiences. Sensitive history taking and adequate medical studies involve much more than the detection or elimination of organic disease; they aid in determining the relative importance of physical disturbance in the genesis of the child's symptoms. The physical examination provides an evaluation of the adequacy of the somatic structures used by the child in coping with daily experiences and some understanding of the influence of disease, injury, congenital defect and developmental difference on this basic equipment. Relatively minor deviations in a child's basic somatic equipment such as mild visual or auditory disturbances are no less significant than gross physical handicaps and neurological disorders in their potential effect on the child's adaptive capacities. Disorders of perception and poor motor coordination may seriously interfere with the child's ability to meet educational and social challenges. Such disorders may occur in a variety of psychiatric disturbances, including brain injury.

The diagnosis of minimal disturbances of central nervous system function may be very difficult. Careful observation of the child in his activities, with special emphasis on his neurophysiological patterns, is more significant diagnostically than the more formal and classical neurological examination. Inadequate neurological appraisal is often related to a lack of awareness of neurophysiological maturational patterns and the effect on them of emotional interplay and experience. A careful history with particular attention to events which might result in brain damage is essential. The psychological test battery may also give valuable clues to the presence of diffuse brain injury. Electroencephalography may be helpful but in its present state of development may confuse the issue unless there is other clinical evidence to confirm the suspicion of central nervous system disorder.

Inspection alone may serve to point up certain physical or physiological developmental differences which are important in some children. Youngsters who reach their physiological puberty at an early, though still normal age, may have a physiologically determined pubertal reaction which is crucial in the behavioral decompensation. The late maturing of some children, with their feelings of difference from their group, may also contribute to their problems.

In the neurophysiological evaluation it is also essential to learn if the child has been receiving drugs or any other medications for the treatment of already existing behavioral disability or some organic illness. Certain drugs may alter the basic behavior patterns of the child, leading at times to depression and hypo-activity or to overactivity, irritability, excitement and even hallucinations. At present such drugs include the "tranquillizers", antihistamines, and endocrine preparations as well as the barbiturates.

The physical assessment of the child calls for mature clinical judgment on the part of the child psychiatrist. He should decide not only whether additional studies are necessary, but also whether they will add to the child's and his family's anxieties and only lead to more confusion. Like the thoughtful physician in all specialties he should determine when further diagnostic procedures are actually justified or merely reflect his own illogical concern. When physical studies are indicated, the child psychiatrist should provide adequate psychological preparation for both the child and his parents. On the other hand, he must avoid unwarranted repetitive examinations under pressures from parents who defensively wish to ascribe some organic etiology to psychogenic problems. At such times it may be imperative for the child psychiatrist to indicate confidently and tactfully his disagreement with the family's "diagnosis." The child psychiatrist's help to the parents may include consultations with the referring physician, or if the child was referred by a non-medical agency, it involves referral to and collaboration with a pediatrician or other medical specialist.

For most effective diagnostic work in a psychiatric clinic the other members of the clinic team should be identified with the nature of the physician's medical function. The medical responsibilities of the child psychiatrist include the collection and synthesis of medical information into a sound appraisal of the child's physical reality, the interpretation of the physical findings to professional colleagues and parents, and their integration into the total evaluation of all the accumulated diagnostic data. As a physician the child psychiatrist through his basic medical training and experience brings to the diagnostic process valuable knowledge about the physical aspects of children's psychiatric disabilities such as the sequelae of infectious disease and about many other interactions between physiological and emotional forces.

C. The Psychological Examination

The psychological examination serves as an aid to the evaluation of the limitations and assets of children who are referred for psychiatric study. Testing is particularly indicated when there are questions involving learning difficulties, mental retardation, the possibility of brain injury, or the existence of psychosis. It has the additional function of helping to obtain a general picture of the child's problem areas and intra-psychic dynamics and occasionally that of evaluating the effects of treatment. Some of the controversy concerning the use of tests in this latter role hinges on the fact that they may be given a large share of the diagnostic and prognostic load without the clinical checks and validation of their findings that a more comprehensive evaluation of diagnosis and treatment can offer. However, whether the psychological examination is used selectively or routinely, it is important to bear in mind certain basic questions, such as: What does the experience of being tested mean to the child? When should children not be tested? How is the child prepared for psychological examination? What do these tests generally measure? What is the role of the psychologist as tester and interpreter? How meaningful are the results? How can the results of testing be put to the best use in helping the child? What is their relation to the psychiatric examination of the child?

The Tests — In most clinics, three types of tests are generally used: intelligence tests, achievement tests and projective tests; and occasionally, measures of aptitude and interest. The Stanford-Binet and the Wechsler Intelligence Scale for Children, and the Wechsler Adult Scale (for adolescents) are most frequently given. All have a high degree of validity when used with children of school age and older. The Binet Test is available for pre-school children down to the age of two, and other tests, such as the Psyche Cattell Infant Tests, the Gesell Scale of Development and the Merrill-Palmer Scales have been devised for infants and pre-school children. The reliability of infants' and young children's tests is comparatively poor in and of themselves exclusive of other studies of the child. In general, it can be said that a high score has more significance and validity than a low score. These tests are often helpful, however, in making gross distinctions between very bright and very dull intelligences. The reliability for prediction of any intelligence test score for a child under the age of 4 or 5 is open to question.

Although performance on an intelligence test is certainly vulnerable to anxiety and emotional upset, the intelligence test gives a better picture than projective tests of the child's assets and of what he can do best. This is true because the intelligence test is structured and because, by the time a child is of school age, the procedure of tapping his knowledge and intellectual functioning is somewhat familiar to him. Unless he is undergoing acute anxiety about the testing situation, in which case he should not be tested, the intelligence test performance yields the more valid insights into the child's capabilities and potentialities, be they meager or abundant.

Achievement tests measure the benefits the child has derived from his educational endeavors. Often the lack of correlation between educational achievement and mental ability uncovers the nature of general learning problems or specific ones such as in reading or arithmetic.

24

Projective tests have in common the presentation of relatively unstructured material to the child so that his responses to the test material are more of a function of his subjective reactions and his internal dynamics than of the test material. Nonetheless, projective tests differ in the degree of the structuring they present, and this difference is important in evaluating test results. Children differ in their ability to tolerate lack of structure, but in general, lack of structure and familiarity tend to arouse anxiety and hostility. Many responses to projective tests are a reflection of the child's conflicts or his defenses against them. Moreover, projective tests permit responses which are of a more primitive and impulse-ridden nature than responses to more structured tasks. Thus, projective tests are prone to stress the conflicts within the child but do not always indicate the clinical significance of the apparent psychopathology. This does not mean that such assets as creativity and ego-strength are not tapped by these tests, but care must be used to avoid overestimating the degree of psychopathology.

Among the projective tests, the Rorschach Ink-Blot Test is the most unstructured and the one most likely to reveal the nuclear conflicts, basic anxieties, and the level of emotional maturation. However, the Rorschach scoring categories do provide some insight into personality functioning inasmuch as the sharpness of reality testing, the nature of the defenses, the degree of anxiety and capacity for emotional control and inner life are among the many aspects of personality structure which can be evaluated. Tests, like the Thematic Apperception Test, the Children's Apperception Test, and the Michigan Picture Test, where the child is asked to tell stories in response to pictures, are more structured, apparently reveal less of the child's instinctual conflicts than the Rorschach Test, and often give a better balanced picture of the child's ego weaknesses and strengths. These picture-story methods focus on the child's defenses or ways of handling interpersonal and social situations; they reveal what he perceives as being the major internal and external forces acting on him and his methods of meeting these needs and forces. The Draw-A-Person Test which is considered a reflection of the child's body-image gives some insight into the child's self-image.

The very nature of the projective tests is in accord with their relative lack of reliability for the pre-school child as compared to the school-age child whose personality is more structured. The different facets of personality which these projective measures tap and the different degrees of pathology they measure point to the need for a battery of tests in order to obtain a well-rounded personality picture. Thus, an intelligence test and a variety of projective tests are necessary to arrive at a useful personality description.

The test battery becomes important, too, in attempting to evaluate brain injury in children. There is no single typical pattern of responses in brain damaged children — usually the psychologist has to make inferences from his test data as to whether brain injury might be present. He is best equipped to make these inferences if he has a backlog of experience and if he has a variety of samples of the child's test behavior. The Binet Test may provide some of this information if there are specific impairments in visual-motor coordination, memory, or certain kinds of abstract tasks. The Bender-Gestalt, a test involving the copying of geometric figures, provides clues when the organization of these figures and their forms are destroyed when the child copies them. Organic brain impairment is often reflected on the Rorschach Test in poorly integrated responses of poor form quality, in an inability to handle color, or in the repetition of certain responses. None of these test signs by itself is a positive indicator, and, in fact, diagnosis of brain injury cannot be made on the basis of the tests alone. Nevertheless, a skilled psychologist if provided with sufficient data, can often pick up enough indications from a battery of psychological tests to suggests the possibility of brain damage.

The validity and meaningfulness of projective test results are very dependent on the skill, the experience and the personality of the psychologist. This, of course, is true to some degree of all tests, but takes on more importance both in the administration and interpretation of projective tests. Often, much of what the patient does on projective tests is a function of the personality of the psychologist and the kind of relationship that has been set up between the child and the tester. This does not invalidate the test results if the tester is sensitive to these effects. Test interpretation is enhanced by this sensitivity on the part of the examiner, but when the sensitivity is lacking, test reports may be distorted.

Contra-Indications for Testing — The decision as to whether a child should or should not be tested depends essentially on two factors: the degree of emotional trauma involved for him and the amount of meaningful information one can glean from his test performance. The first, of course, is the more important. A test is never so important that a child should have to undergo severe anxiety or panic because of it. Sometimes this can be ascertained beforehand with the information one has concerning the child's typical reaction to tests, new situations and new people. The psychologist must be sensitive to signs that might indicate that too much strain is being placed on the child and frequently testing may have to be postponed until treatment is well under way. A child should not be subjected to an over-fatiguing experience, and testing may have to be stopped to meet the child's needs. Young children, especially, cannot be kept for overly-long periods. Negativistic children, acting-out children, the very distractible and very disturbed are not good subjects for valid testing. Sometimes the skill of the tester can overcome some of these drawbacks, or testing can often be accomplished at a later date. Frequently a good psychologist can obtain bits of information concerning the child's intellectual functioning and typical defensive patterns from the fragmentary testing he can accomplish with a disturbed or resistive child.

If psychological examinations are to fulfill their purpose, they should be of some assistance to the child in helping him to meet his problems. Psychological examinations are not ends in themselves, but are aids to the child, his parents, and the clinic team in their endeavors to find ways and means of resolving difficulties. Most frequently test results are used by the psychiatrist and social worker as another source of information to be used as a guide in dealing with parents and child. The information may corroborate what is already known or add new information. In any event, its purpose remains that of helping to answer the question of "how can we best help the child?"

D. The Psychiatric Examination

The child psychiatrist brings to the diagnostic process his medical and psychiatric knowledge of the whole spectrum of human behavior whereby he sees personality development as a continuum from infancy through childhood, adolescence and adulthood. He uses his appreciation of what is expected of and appropriate for boys and girls of varying ages and social settings. He is aware that the mere collection of biographic and psychodynamic detail does not yield an understanding of a particular symptomatology or of specific psychopathology.

Before he sees the child, the psychiatrist has interviewed the parents or familiarized himself with the information (nature and history of the problem, the child's developmental history, the emotional climate of the home, etc.) already obtained by other professional colleagues. This briefing provides him with working hypotheses about the child's difficulties and some expectation of what he will find in his diagnostic interviews. It is his task to create an emotional setting within which he and the child may interact so that the youngster can express his needs and concerns and the psychiatrist, in his turn, perceives how the child relates to an adult in a new and stressful situation. At the same time, he maintains a certain distance, seeking to give the child a sense of "having room to move around in". Through his disciplined awareness of the child's anxiety as well as the emotional level at which he functions, the psychiatrist provides understanding and an appropriate realistic responsiveness. Within the framework of this relationship he can observe and appraise the child's behavior patterns which reflect both his feelings and his adaptive capacities. These can then be evaluated in terms of the child's expected emotional, intellectual and physical maturity and in light of the pertinent data from the personal history.

The examination of the child really begins in the waiting room, where the psychiatrist meets and briefly welcomes the child and his parents, utilizing this opportunity to note the interaction between parents and child and their anticipatory attitudes about the coming session. He can then observe the child's physical appearance and note any striking resemblances or lack of them to the parents. The ease or difficulty with which the child can separate from his parents to go with the physician to the office is often extremely revealing of both the parent-child relationship and the child's degree of differentiation from his mother and father. The child or the parents may suffer from marked separation anxiety, and it may be well in that case to allow all of them to go to the interviewing room for at least a few minutes. If the child and parents are helped to tolerate their anxiety, this obvious respect for their separation fears will prove an important step in their being able to overcome them.

It is desirable that the interviewing room be set up to provide the child with a reasonable balance of freedom and protection and to offer simple play materials appropriate to his age, affording both creative and aggressive expression. Physical examining rooms or luxurious adult offices rarely afford an appropriate setting for a psychiatric session with a young child. He should not be expected to sit quietly in a chair the entire time, and he may be quite reassured to have the bathroom pointed out to him on the way to the office. As the child goes along with the psychiatrist some spontaneous comments about reality matters such as the trip to the clinic or office, the child's school or an incident in the waiting room may help to allay his anxiety about the separation from his parents and facilitate his perception of the psychiatrist as a responsive human being.

As the two settle down in the office the psychiatrist often finds it helpful in establishing a mutual understanding to inquire about the child's ideas of the reasons for his visit. Even more important will be the child's feelings about the visit, even though he may not be able to express them freely at this time. Almost all children who come to a clinic require some clarification of the kind of place it is, the troubles children may have that bring them there and the roles of the different persons he and his parents see. Many children fear that the "doctor will give them needles or medicine", and it is worthwhile for the psychiatrist to spend a few minutes talking of the kind of doctor he is, and of the ways in which he can help the child. The precise technique of the initial as well as the later stages of the psychiatric evaluation of the child will naturally vary with the individual, his age, and the nature of his difficulties, as well as with the personality and skill of the psychiatrist, and cannot be particularized in this brief report.

Fairly early in the first interview a child should receive some orientation about the likely duration of the session and the number of such sessions and about other procedures as the psychological testing or neurological examination. One cannot assume that any child will automatically trust an adult who is strange to him, and some children who come to a clinic feel that they have many reasons for mistrusting adults in general. The child patient may expect and fear that all he does and says will be reported to his parents and the psychiatrist should make it clear that if he does talk with them, he will tell the child about the purpose and nature of their conversation.

Except with the very young or severely disturbed child, early discussion of his home, the members of his family, his friends or interests will often facilitate a productive relationship between the child and the psychiatrist and will give the latter some insight into the areas of the child's life which are gratifying as well as those in which he is experiencing difficulty. The way in which he talks of himself and his life may reveal his anxieties, fears and conflicts as well as his modes of dealing with them. Strong resistances against facing his feelings and problems and against change may be clearly reflected in such an interchange.

Play activities suitable for his age and interest can be suggested to foster the interchange and to elucidate further those areas of conflict which are unconscious to him and his methods of protecting himself against becoming aware of them. His capacity to utilize modes of symbolic communication, his expression of fantasy preoccupation and the ways in which he involves the psychiatrist in his play are important clues in evaluating his conflicts, defenses and capacity to change. Whether he asks to play or begins to play spontaneously, as well as his selection of play materials, whether drawing, painting, writing stories, modeling clay or play with toy soldiers, should be noted. Play activities provide an opportunity for participation of the psychiatrist if the child wishes it.

While the nature of the participation of the psychiatrist in the diagnostic sessions with the child is admittedly difficult to define, the phrase, "receptive participant", expresses as well as any the appropriate attitude in which the psychiatrist lets the child take the lead while he interacts responsively with his young patient. The diagnostician who leaves all initiative to an uncertain, uneasy child may increase his patient's anxiety to an undesirable degree. On the other hand, one who presents his young patient with set play situations and stereotyped questions may fail to elicit nuances of reaction and spontaneous behavior which contain important clues to the child's anxieties or to his defensive operations. The fact that a psychiatrist is carrying out a diagnostic study and may see

30

the child but a few times makes it important that he follow certain technical limitations. The number of diagnostic sessions may vary from one to five or six. One interview may give an initial impression but usually three or four at weekly intervals provide the most favorable opportunity for observation of the child and are less likely to provoke an intense relationship difficult for the child to give up, than the maximum of five or six. It is usually possible to achieve a working appraisal during the diagnostic study which is at the same time a constructive and gratifying experience for the young patient. Above all the psychiatrist seeks to avoid mobilizing excessive anxiety or guilt feelings with which the child may have no help in the immediate future.

In these interviews the psychiatrist's attitude should facilitate the child's perception of him as an interested, responsible adult whose greater size and strength will be used willingly in the child's best interests, if necessary, by actively controlling the situation when the child's impulses and anxieties get out of bounds. Precisely because the child's visits may be limited in number, his defenses should be respected and any suggestion of seduction into forbidden activity avoided. It may be particularly important to limit the child's destructive or regressive behavior during the sessions and it is rarely necessary for information purposes, nor advantageous to the patient to permit acting out behavior to go unchecked. How the child responds to such limitation is in itself a diagnostic clue. The psychiatrist may also need to protect the child by guarding him from activities which will bring punishment and disapproval from the parents.

Usually it is well for the psychiatrist to bring up in due time the parents' reasons for the visits if the child has not discussed them. If it is obvious that the topic is highly charged, that the child is too ashamed or frightened to talk of his bed-wetting or fire-setting for example, it may be preferable not to press him for details since the relationship may be a brief one. However, total silence from the psychiatrist concerning the child's problem is rarely reassuring to him and may only serve to reinforce the denials which the child and perhaps his family use to cope with his behavior.

The child may change considerably in his behavior, mood and relationship to the psychiatrist during the diagnostic study.

However, unless the psychiatrist has forced his own impress upon the sessions, the three or four interviews with the child will display a certain continuity, with consistent themes and elaborations, characteristic expressions of anxiety and ways of handling it. A sense of the child's style should emerge, a sketch of the main outlines of his personality, the nature of his problems and his habitual modes of dealing with them.

E. The Diagnostic Formulation

From the diagnostic examinations described above an initial understanding of the child's problem gradually emerges. Each individual examiner arrives at some tentative hypothesis based on the data obtained from his specialized observations and studies which he evaluates within the framework of the knowledge of his own discipline. From his own point of view he collects and objectively describes his findings, summarizes them into generalizations and sifts out any inconsistencies. Within the structure of his theoretical concepts, he searches for correlations between the child's problems and his clinical findings, and he makes some speculations concerning dynamic and causal factors. Within each investigative area this synthesis of the diagnostic material becomes an important though incomplete aspect of the diagnostic thinking.

The comprehensive diagnosis of the total child-in-his-environment involves the integration of the various syntheses achieved by the separate examiners. It consists of accumulating all the clinical evidence and weighing the multiple factors against each other. Valid findings complement and corroborate each other and fit together like the parts of a puzzle into the outlines of a meaningful whole picture. However, any discrepancies and conflicting evidence point to a need for delineating more precisely the areas in which they occur and for enlarging the dynamic understanding either through further studies or in an on-going diagnostic-treatment process.

The initial diagnostic formulation is derived from this total diagnostic process. It serves a valuable purpose although it yields only incomplete insights rather than final answers. Its aim is to provide a sound working diagnosis leading to a valid prognosis and a practical course of action in dealing with the presenting problem.

The diagnostic formulation is achieved in the psychiatric clinic through the collaborative efforts of the child psychiatrist and other medical and non-medical professional personnel. In other settings the psychiatrist may work with fewer colleagues, or in private practice may work alone in gathering and evaluating data. Whatever the setting, the nature, scope and purpose of the diagnostic study remain the same. In traditional clinic practice, the formulation of the diagnosis is facilitated by the procedure of having a diagnostic conference following the completion of the several examinations. Each professional worker summarizes the strengths and weaknesses of the child and his environment as they have been discovered and substantiated in the course of his investigation. On the basis of his knowledge and experience each also presents for further exploration his own impressions for which the evidence is still inconclusive as well as any areas about which no information is available. Thus, each examiner contributes to the understanding of the multiple physical, psychological and social aspects of the problem. This understanding is then summarized into a comprehensive clinical-dynamic-genetic diagnosis, which is much more than the mere descriptive labelling of clinical signs and symptoms.

Nosological classifications, which in themselves are incomplete, are only the beginning of the diagnostic formulation. Nevertheless, as convenient clinical shorthand they cannot be ignored since they have some place in the development of theoretical concepts and in the establishment of psychiatric treatment services. The diagnosis of a clinical entity such as conversion hysteria, schizophrenia or a post-encephalitic syndrome is not only helpful in determining the immediate practical management of the patient but is essential for statistical purposes. When it is based on a thorough knowledge of general and childhood psychopathology, it may also afford significant leads for investigating pertinent dynamic-genetic factors. However, care must be exercised in using these clinical classifications of children's disabilities because sometimes parents, physicians and community agencies misunderstand and misuse such labels to the detriment of the child. Nosological classifications actually label only the pathology and do not include the child's and his family's assets. Whenever possible a clinical diagnosis should be made, but with children in a developmental state, such classification is often difficult since the clinical entities are not clearly defined.

This Committee believes that further work on the delineation of clinical classifications related to developmental stages in childhood and to the interaction of the child and his environment is an essential step in the growing field of child psychiatry.

Diagnosis is first a clinical-dynamic evaluation or a current cross-sectional formulation of the presenting problem in its total context. Such understanding includes an assessment of the area and degree of the disability, of the environmental stresses, of the strengths of the child and his family, and of the specific ego patterns used in current relationships with others, including the clinic staff. It takes into account the readiness of both the child and his parents for help. The interplay of the child and his parents with the clinic staff includes not only certain realistic aspects of the situation but also some illogical displacements from current and past significant relationships. These transference attitudes are reviewed in the light of and correlated with historical data concerning emotional responses to former key people and events, including reactive patterns to developmental experiences. This leads to a second important aspect of total diagnosis, the reconstruction of a longitudinal or dynamic-genetic diagnosis. It is a formulation of the interplay of the multiple sources of conflict and anxiety as they have arisen in the past throughout the entire course of development. The dynamic diagnosis is a clarification of what the patient does and how he interacts with his environment; the genetic diagnosis is an interpretation of why he responds as he does and where and how his problems originated. Without such dynamic-genetic understanding sound treatment plans cannot be established, and the staff of a psychiatric treatment facility cannot function as a cohesive unit in its service to the child and his parents.

Implicit in the clinic's approach to diagnosis is the conviction of the importance of the involvement of the parents from the very beginning of the dynamic diagnostic process. For future help to the child and parents it is desirable that the family and the clinical staff arrive at the diagnostic summary period with sufficient mutual understanding to make it likely that the family is ready and able to continue a relationship with the clinic, if treatment is recommended.

In this early stage, such comprehensive diagnostic formulation is only an initial, partial dynamic evaluation, which is, neverthe-

34

less, necessary for planning treatment. It may later be revised or reinforced and elaborated since diagnostic thinking continues throughout the whole course of treatment. The diagnostic process provides experiences for the child and his parents which often constitute a sound beginning for treatment. In itself it has therapeutic value for many families, and this potential is more apt to be realized when the diagnostic procedures are carried out in a treatment setting.

IV. TREATMENT GOALS, PLANS AND PROGNOSIS

Comprehensive treatment evolves directly from the diagnostic formulation which gives purpose and direction to therapeutic goals, prognostic speculations, and appropriate plans to ameliorate or correct the child's emotional disability. The plan will vary depending on the child's needs, the family relationships and potentialities as well as on the resources within the community and clinic. The choice of professional personnel to carry out the treatment plan requires consideration of the training, experience, skills and personality of the available staff members.

Treatment goals and methods are planned individually for each child and his family according to the specific dynamic-genetic diagnosis. Since the nature of the symptoms alone does not reflect the severity of the underlying disturbances or the degree to which the child's development is blocked, this procedure is followed whether the symptoms are minimal or marked and regardless of the frequency of similar presenting problems in other children. For example, the need for an individual approach is clearly understood when the child psychiatrist is confronted with planning treatment for children who present the rather common symptom of enuresis. The treatment plan for the child whose lifetime enuresis is primarily associated with severe mental deficiency or neurological disease will be very different from that which is recommended for the persistently enuretic child who manifests no significant internal disorder but lives in a large sub-standard family of several bedwetters where little if any stimulation or assistance is given the child for learning appropriate habits of cleanliness. Treatment will differ too for the child who was previously toilet-trained, perhaps by complying prematurely to rigid demands, and who later regressed to bed-wetting when his basic anxieties were reactivated by insurmountable life situations.

In each instance the attempt is made to devise specific treatment measures. However, only too frequently the treatment plan of choice cannot be put into effect because of limited community and clinic resources. In this event an alternative plan with a more limited goal may have to be followed. This Committee believes that an ideal plan of treatment should be constructed and recorded whenever possible along with the reasons which necessitate the adoption of a less-desirable plan of action. This procedure would foster the development of diagnostic skills, sound judgment and flexibility in planning treatment. In addition it would provide valuable documentary data for evaluating existing services and for demonstrating the need for improved child care and therapeutic facilities.

The individual treatment plan may include a variety of direct and indirect methods. Occasionally only one type is indicated, centering primarily on physical, social or psychological factors. For example, the treatment for one child with a learning problem is the direct medical treatment of his visual defect; for another it is direct work with the child in remedial reading; while for a third it consists of an indirect environmental approach by effecting an appropriate grade placement in school. More often the plan of action involves both indirect and direct procedures and deals with multiple inter-related facets of the child's personality and his environment. For a mentally defective child, the plan may encompass direct medical treatment, specialized education with vocational training while living at home or in institutional placement, and perhaps psychotherapy to help the child resolve some of his inevitable internal conflicts. It includes work with the parents, often social casework services, to help them face both the negative and positive factors in the situation and to prepare them to take the next steps constructively.

Indirect treatment of the child solely through casework or psychiatric treatment for the parents is frequently the preferred plan when the child's anxiety has not yet been internalized and when his problem occurs transitionally in response to the parents' inappropriate attitudes and child care methods. Such a reactive disability may represent prolonged or exaggerated conflicts specific to a particular developmental stage which the child has difficulty in resolving because of the parents' illogical expectations. For these children, treatment is geared to helping the significant parent or both parents to understand the developmental problem and to handle it more constructively. This method is often effective in dealing with the problems of the very young child, but a hopeful prognosis is predicated on an accurate evaluation of the parents' capacity to modify their interactions with the child.

When a child has developed marked intra-psychic conflicts and emotional disabilities which cannot be alleviated by parental treatment alone or by some other environmental modification, the treatment plan includes direct psychotherapy for the child. Within a therapeutic relationship with an interested, understanding, relatively mature adult, a corrective emotional experience is provided. Depending on the nature and degree of the child's psychopathology and strengths, varying intensities of therapeutic work in particular areas of conflict might be indicated. The specific psychotherapeutic methods may range from supportive relationship therapy alone to several kinds and levels of dynamic insight therapy, including psychoanalytic child psychotherapy and child psychoanalysis. They may be planned to emphasize one or more aspects of the treatment process: the abreaction of feeling while the child is revealing directly or symbolically his conflicts and defenses; the working through of inner conflicts within the relationship by the development of some insight through the clarification of dynamic patterns and the interpretation of genetic factors; and the strengthening of ego functions through re-education and through the ultimate resolution of illogical attitudes in the therapeutic relationship.

Regardless of its level or intensity, effective psychotherapy for the child requires the participation of the parent or parents. For example, the ultimate prognosis for achieving continued masculine development in a passive inhibited boy depends largely upon the concomitant help to the parents in overcoming their restrictive infantalizing attitudes and faulty identifications as the child himself is helped to become more active. This collaborative parent-child treatment, which is frequently the plan of choice, constitutes a unique contribution of the American child psychiatric clinic. In many clinics, work with parents has traditionally been the function of the psychiatric social worker. The prognosis in collaborative treatment is largely determined by the flexibility and strength of the several family members who are involved in the therapeutic plan.

It also depends on the skills of the psychiatrists, psychiatric social workers, and clinical psychologists and on available time and opportunity for them to work together closely in integrating their cumulative insights and in developing further their methods and goals in the continuous diagnostic-treatment process.

Occasionally the parents' active participation in a collaborative treatment process is contra-indicated because of their lack of motivation and capacity to change or because their modification might be detrimental to the child's improvement or the family's welfare. This occurs when parental patterns protect them from psychoses by maintaining some equilibrium, albeit pathological, within the family. In these instances, direct psychotherapy with the child alone has a very poor prognosis; and even with attempts to foster healthier identifications and improved adaptations outside the family, direct psychotherapy still demands an unreasonable degree of self-sufficiency on the part of the child. Moreover, significant improvement by the child might seriously disrupt the tenuous family balance. Although older adolescents can occasionally be helped without the continued active participation of the parents this is rarely if ever true for the younger child, whose further development still depends largely on his parents. Even with adolescents in the less seriously disturbed families, parental interest and support and at least their cooperation and agreement to the treatment plan for the child are required.

When intensely disturbed family relationships prevent the child and parents from engaging constructively in a collaborative treatment process, the child's separation from the family is sometimes recommended as a temporary measure to facilitate treatment opportunities for both the child and his parents. As a necessary adjunct to psychotherapy the child may require a corrective living experience in the therapeutic milieu of an inpatient psychiatric treatment facility. Some parents, relieved of the stress of the everyday care of the disturbed child, have greater energies and motivation to face their own involvements and to modify their responses to the child. Inpatient psychiatric treatment for the child with actively participating parents facilitates the development of sound parent-child collaborative treatment. The goal is the child's return to his own home in a happier, more stable family relationship which will foster his continued emotional growth.

When parents lack the capacity or motivation for participation, whether the child is treated on an inpatient or outpatient basis, the child's placement outside the home might be recommended in order to offer the child a more supportive environment and the opportunity to benefit from such other treatment measures as might be indicated. The placement recommendation should be based on the child's particular needs. It should indicate whether a foster home, boarding home, resident school, a special type of inpatient psychiatric unit or other institution is desirable. Only too frequently a specific plan cannot be carried out because of the dearth of appropriate facilities. Often the parents are unable to accept separation from the child. At all times, collaborative work in preparing the child and parents for placement is the clinic's responsibility in the treatment plan in cooperation with appropriate community agencies. Sometimes when placement is more desirable but cannot be effected, the diagnostic formulation offers some reasonable basis for trying the traditional methods of outpatient collaborative treatment. At other times it is folly to proceed with treatment while the child remains in the home. In extreme situations when the child's welfare demands placement outside the home it may be necessary to bring the child's plight to the attention of the official child welfare agency or court.

Other social modifications are frequently recommended as major or adjunctive aspects of a treatment plan. Diagnostic study may reveal that the child's disability represents a direct reaction to parental anxieties associated with difficult experiences such as financial insecurity or serious family illness. In such cases the treatment plan is geared to the correction of the family problem by referral to appropriate community resources. At other times children themselves are helped through environmental modification with or without direct psychotherapy. Community recreational facilities, organized club activities and day nurseries offer normal group experience and opportunity for developing skills and healthy behavior patterns. Special educational facilities are sometimes indicated. Teachers serve as significant adult figures for the child. Moreover their observations of child behavior can be helpful to the psychiatric facility which in turn can offer them support and understanding of the child's problems.

A vital step in treatment planning is the discussion with the parents of what they and the clinic have learned during the diagnostic process. It includes an appropriate explanation of the clinical findings and recommendations as well as a review of the understanding which the parents have gained about themselves, especially in relation to their children. Insights acquired by the parents in the initial diagnostic study often have a significant therapeutic potential. However, many parents may require further help in clarifying their motivations or in overcoming their resistances to the recommended treatment plan. Treatment planning also includes the appropriate interpretation of the diagnostic formulation and recommendations to the referring person or agency. This communication is a basic medical responsibility.

In conclusion, while this report has described the diagnostic process in a psychiatric clinic for children, the Committee wishes to re-emphasize that the same careful consideration of the child and his setting is indispensable wherever child psychiatry is practiced. The effectiveness of any treatment plan recommended for an emotionally disabled child evolves from a sound diagnostic appraisal.

SUGGESTED REFERENCES

The following references have been chosen as examples of the excellent body of literature available on topics pertinent to this report. The Committee thinks that these selections should be helpful in illustrating the broad range of material which is relevant to the understanding of the diagnostic process in child psychiatry.

Ackerman, N. W. "Psychiatric Disorders in Children, Diagnosis and Etiology in Our Time". CURRENT PROBLEMS IN PSYCHIATRIC DIAGNOSIS. Paul H. Hoch and Joseph Zubin, eds. Grune and Stratton, 1953.

———— and Behrens, Marjorie H. "Child and Family Psychopathy: Problems of Correlation". PSYCHOPATHOLOGY OF CHILDHOOD. Paul H. Hoch and Joseph Zubin, eds. pp. 177-196. Grune and Stratton, 1955.

———— "Interlocking Pathology in Family Relationships". CHANGING CONCEPTS IN PSYCHOANALYTIC MEDICINE. S. Rado and G. E. Daniels, eds. Grune and Stratton, 1956.

Allen, Frederick H. PSYCHOTHERAPY WITH CHILDREN. Norton, 1942.

Benda, C. E. et al. "The Inadequacy of Present-Day Concepts of Mental Deficiency and Mental Illness in Child Psychiatry". *Am. J. Psychiat.*, 107:721-729, 1951.

Bender, Lauretta. CHILD PSYCHIATRIC TECHNIQUES. C. C. Thomas, 1952.

Benedek, Therese. "The Psychosomatic Implications of the Primary Unit: Mother-Child". *Am. J. Ortho.* XIX, 642, 1949.

Doll, E. A. "The Feeble-Minded Child". Ch. 17, MANUAL OF CHILD PSYCHOLOGY. Leonard Carmichael, ed. John Wiley & Sons, Inc., 1946.

Erikson, Erik H. CHILDHOOD AND SOCIETY. W. W. Norton, 1950.

Freud, Sigmund. THE EGO AND THE ID. Hogarth Press, 1927.

———— "Three Contributions to the Theory of Sex". THE BASIC WRITINGS OF SIGMUND FREUD. pp. 553-629. Modern Library, 1938.

———— INHIBITIONS, SYMPTOMS AND ANXIETY. Hogarth Press, 1936.

Freud, Anna. THE EGO AND MECHANISMS OF DEFENSE. Hogarth Press, 1937.

———— THE PSYCHOANALYTICAL TREATMENT OF CHILDREN. Imago, 1946.

———— et al (ed.). THE PSYCHOANALYTIC STUDY OF THE CHILD. Vols. I-XI. International University Press, 1945-1956.

Gardner, George (ed.). CASE STUDIES IN CHILDHOOD EMOTIONAL DIS-ABILITES. Vol. I., Vol. II. American Ortho. Ass'n, 1953, 1956.

Gerard, Margaret. "Emotional Disorders of Childhood". Ch. VII, DYNAMIC PSYCHIATRY. F. Alexander and H. Ross, eds. University of Chicago Press, 1952.

Goodenough, Florence L. "The Measurement of Mental Growth in Childhood". MANUAL OF CHILD PSYCHOLOGY. Leonard Carmichael, ed. Ch. 9, pp. 450-475. John Wiley & Sons, Inc., 1946.

Group for the Advancement of Psychiatry. BASIC CONCEPTS IN CHILD PSYCHIATRY. Formulated by The Committee on Child Psychiatry. Report 12, April, 1950.

——————— INTEGRATION AND CONFLICT IN FAMILY BEHAVIOR. Formulated by the Committee on the Family. Report 27, August, 1954.

Josselyn, Irene. PSYCHOSOCIAL DEVELOPMENT OF CHILDREN. Family Service Ass'n of America, 1948.

Kanner, L., CHILD PSYCHIATRY. C. C. Thomas, 1948.

Levine, Maurice. "Principles of Psychiatric Treatment". DYNAMIC PSYCHI-ATRY, Ch. XI. F. Alexander and H. Ross, eds. University of Chicago Press, 1952.

Lippman, Hyman. TREATMENT OF THE CHILD IN EMOTIONAL CONFLICT. McGraw-Hill, 1956.

Lowrey, L. G. (ed.). ORTHOPSYCHIATRY 1923-1948: RETROSPECT AND PROSPECT. Amer. Ortho. Ass'n, 1948.

Pearson, Gerard. EMOTIONAL DISORDERS OF CHILDREN. W. W. Norton, 1949.

——————— PSYCHOANALYSIS AND THE EDUCATION OF THE CHILD. W. W. Norton, 1954.

Piaget, Jean. THE LANGUAGE AND THOUGHT OF THE CHILD. Harcourt Brace & Co., 1932.

Rambert, Madeleine. CHILDREN IN CONFLICT. Int'l Univ. Press, 1949.

Rank, Beata. "Adaptation of the Psychoanalytic Technique for the Treatment of Young Children With Atypical Development". Am. J. Ortho., 19:130, 1949.

Selye, Hans. THE STRESS OF LIFE. McGraw-Hill, 1956.

Szurek, S. A. "An Attitude Towards (Child) Psychiatry". Quarterly J. Child Behavior, 1:22-51, 178-213, 375-399, 401-423, 1949.

Van Amerongen, Suzanne. "Initial Psychiatric Family Studies". Am. J. Ortho., 24:78-83, 1954.

Witmer, H. L. PSYCHIATRIC INTERVIEWS WITH CHILDREN. Commonwealth Fund, 1946

Young, Leontine. "Diagnosis as a Creative Process". Social Casework, Vol. XXXVII, No. 6, p. 275. June, 1956.

FROM DIAGNOSIS

TO TREATMENT

IN CHILD PSYCHIATRY

PREFACE

In this book, the Group for the Advancement of Psychiatry Committee on Child Psychiatry plans to discuss differential treatment planning as it has evolved from psychiatric knowledge and experience accumulated over the past fifty years from the diagnosis and treatment of mentally disordered and emotionally disturbed children and their families. Since the report addresses itself to a consideration of the sick child, the topics of prevention and early intervention, primarily directed at the healthy child, will receive only cursory attention.

A publication on treatment planning is a logical escalation in the series of GAP reports issued by the Committee on Child Psychiatry. These began with Report No. 12, BASIC CONCEPTS IN CHILD PSYCHIATRY, followed by Report No. 38, THE DIAGNOSTIC PROCESS, and Report No. 62, PSYCHOPATHOLOGICAL DISORDERS IN CHILDHOOD: A PROPOSED CLASSIFICATION. It is the Committee's ultimate intention to bring these together with the present report and Report No. 21, THE CONTRIBUTION OF CHILD PSYCHIATRY TO PEDIATRIC TREATMENT AND PRACTICE, so as to constitute a basic textbook of child psychiatry.

We recognize that a great deal of treatment planning is carried out in nonmedical settings, not under the direct aegis of physicians. The needs of children are widespread and of considerable magnitude, and we are therefore addressing ourselves to all those working with disturbed children. For this reason, we have intentionally made use of generalizable rather

47

than particular terms and titles such as *clinician, practitioner, coordinator, planner,* and so forth, indicating that different disciplines may be subsumed under these rubrics.

As in the quotation from Bacon at the beginning of the second chapter, we have not pursued originality for its own sake but have tried to put together *for the first time* and in a comprehensive form the scattered ideas from an area of practice that has been taken too much for granted. Our concern, therefore, has been to make manifest what has previously gained expression only in the unorganized, fragmented intuitions and workaday habits of experienced clinicians.

We are aware that it may seem illogical to write a treatise on treatment planning prior to a study of treatment itself. However, the evaluation of treatment in psychiatry is fraught with methodological problems, and the urgent needs of disturbed children cannot afford to wait until these have been solved. We are consequently making the important and, in our view, justifiable assumption that psychiatric treatment for children can, in many cases, be helpful. We would note, nevertheless, that the next report of the Committee will deal with the treatment process.

We also know that there are those who have a professional preference for a certain type of family approach and who speak in holistic terms of family process, family pathology and family therapy. As child psychiatrists, we regard ourselves as strongly family oriented, with a dual focus on the child as an individual on the one side and the child as a member of a closely knit group on the other. Thus we tend to look on the child as having a life to live, both inwardly and outwardly, that is not always submerged in the family. At the same time, we are also mindful of his dependence on the other family members for a large number of his basic needs. The general frame of reference is therefore that of child psychiatry and not family psychiatry.

The discerning reader will no doubt notice that a spirit of

optimism pervades the text in spite of many expressed doubts and concerns. This is characteristic of child psychiatrists in their daily practice. They are inclined to go about their work with much more hopefulness than the circumstances will often warrant. In large measure this is due to the fact that they are dealing with individuals during the plastic and changeable phases of the life cycle when the developmental forces often work hand in glove with the therapist. Child psychiatrists experience and expect more dramatic changes than their colleagues in adult psychiatry.

As with our other GAP reports, this review of differential treatment planning is not intended as an end in itself but as a stimulus to further work in the same field.

1

HISTORICAL INTRODUCTION

> *In [medicine], nothing is required but assiduous and accurate observation, and a good Understanding to direct the proper application of such observation. But to cure the diseases of the Mind, there is required that intimate knowledge of the Human Heart, which must be drawn from life itself, and which books can never teach, of the various disguises, under which Vice recommends herself to the Imagination, the art for association of Ideas which she forms there, the many nameless circumstances that soften the Heart and render it accessible, the Arts of insinuation and persuasion, the Art of breaking false associations of Ideas, or inducing counter associations, and employing one Passion against another; and when such a knowledge is acquired, the successful application of it to practice depends in a considerable degree on powers which no extent of Understanding can confer.*
>
> John Gregory, M.D. (1765)

The precursor of all science is magic. It is therefore not surprising that the prehistory of treatment planning in child psychiatry is steeped in irrational appraisals and unrealistic expectations of what moral, educational or religious measures might accomplish. The first logical step to treatment planning is adequate diagnostic evaluation and, historically, the same causal connection holds. It was only after the child had been recognized as a psychological entity in himself and prone to a wide spectrum of psychological disturbances that subsequent therapeutic strategies could be envisaged and brought into action.

Diagnostic evaluation, as delineated in our Report No. 62 on the classification of psychopathological disorders in childhood, gave some indication of the progress that has been made in this area in the last few decades. The functional disturbances of childhood were not distinguished prior to the present century. Despert,[1] after a careful historical survey, could find no evidence of the concept of emotional illness in children, as understood today, before the mid-nineteenth century, and she concluded that "emotional disturbance in the child is properly a twentieth century phenomenon." In fact, the term *emotional disturbance* was not used with respect to children until 1925. It is especially surprising for us today—when our world, as Aries[2] remarks, "is obsessed by the physical, moral and sexual problems of children"—that there could have been a time when children were not supposed to suffer from any psychiatric complaint other than mental deficiency.

In the first 45 volumes of the *American Journal of Insanity,* published from 1844 on, not a single article dealt specifically with insanity in children.[3] Neurosis, having generally more covert expression, had an even harder time finding a place for itself in the diagnostic manuals and it was not until Freud's[4] detailed clinical description in 1909 of a phobia in a five-year-old boy that the intangibles of neurosis were separated from willfulness and naughtiness. With characteristic boldness, Freud declared that troubles of this kind in childhood were "quite extraordinarily frequent" but were generally "shouted down in the nursery." He advised clinicians that when a mother complained her child's "nerves" were in a bad state, in nine cases out of ten it was likely he was suffering from some form of psychoneurotic anxiety in the process of crystallizing into a phobia.

The history of the treatment of psychological disorders in childhood is similar to the history of their diagnosis. As diagnostic evaluations increased in subtlety and complexity, so treatments multiplied and gained in sophistication. The development of therapeutic measures, however, was not as linear and some effective early treatments were mysteriously consigned to oblivion. Thus, at the end of the eighteenth century, Itard [5] instituted a treatment plan for "the wild boy of Aveyron" that would still be regarded in many ways as valid procedure today. With classic simplicity, the plan had six principal goals and the measures were based on careful diagnostic observation. Itard proposed to give his patient a rudimentary sense of identity by giving him a name with which he might identify; to interest him in social life by making it pleasanter than the one he had left; to awaken his sensibility by stimulating him physically and emotionally; to extend his range of ideas by increasing his needs and contacts; to get him to speak by exercising his capacity for imitation under pressure; and finally, to get him thinking in terms of problem solving by exploiting the child's compulsive need to keep everything in his environment "just so." It was a treatment plan without parents and therefore lacked a vital component to complete success. In time, it became abundantly clear that parents could make or break the best-laid therapeutic schemes and that it was essential to involve them in the planning at all stages.

Itard's work was soon forgotten. As Seguin, his great successor, pointed out, it was "not enough for an idea to be ripe in the mind of a thinker, and to be hailed by the advocates of progress; the social medium in which it falls must be prepared for it as well; otherwise no production ensues from their contact." In fact, there was only very limited production for the next hundred years, when an insightful pioneer, Leonard Guthrie, laid the groundwork for the therapeutic approach and orientation characterizing the latter part of the nineteenth century.

Guthrie,[6] anticipating Freud, found it hard to understand and accept the exclusion of physicians from the psychological

care of children. "If children were ill or ailing, the doctor
was called upon to prescribe for their diseases, but advice on
their management in general was neither sought nor welcomed.
He was not asked to see a child because it was wayward, but
because it was wasting, not because it was dainty, capricious in
appetite, refusing food considered good for it, and craving
for all that is unwholesome, but because it had pains in its
stomach. Advice was not asked for peevish, passionate children,
nor for those who were afraid of the dark, and unnaturally
timid, absent-minded, or brooding and morose, jealous, spiteful,
or cruel, nor for mischievous, untruthful, dishonest, or immoral
children. All such defects were regarded as moral rather than
morbid, and were treated as such." Using surprisingly con-
temporary language, he also complained of "the tendency to
lay too much stress upon the actual complaint from which a
child suffers and not enough upon the child's personality and
environment," and to overlook the fact that "if a child is
miserable, its health, like that of an adult, suffers; the cause of
the misery may seem trivial, but its effect upon health may be
prolonged throughout its life." He said that it should not
always be assumed that unfortunate parents were to blame for
a child's disturbance. "The neurotic child may disagree with
his surroundings and not the surroundings with the child."

In prescribing treatment for the emotionally disturbed
child, Guthrie insisted that there were important principles to
be remembered. The professional armamentarium was no
longer confined to medicines for coughs, worms, stomach aches,
and fits. One had often to dispense "more platitudes than
pills" but if these were based on common sense and common
knowledge, they need not be despised. It was wrong to recommend punishment for emotionally upset children, since they
were already overburdened with the punishment from guilt.
He was the first to point out that children in the hospital
suffered from "hospitalism" and that the slum child preferred
his primitive, drunken mother to the happy, comfortable

hospital. Bromides might be good for neurotic children; they acted even better when they were given, he said, to the parents. He especially warned against the policy of continuous repression of emotional display, as practiced by Mrs. Wesley, who prided herself on having taught her baby to "cry quietly." Guthrie's golden rules for the management of emotionally disturbed children had little effect on practitioners. Once again the social medium was not ready. It was psychoanalysis, a few years later, which created the emotional climate that set the sequential process of diagnosis and treatment moving again.[7]

In 1909, the first modern child guidance clinic in the United States was set up by Healy and his co-workers, and the child psychiatric patient at long last began to receive the specialized attention previously denied him. The child, and his family, were now confronted by a team of experts who carefully considered both their internal and their external world, their past and present lives. The child, for the first time in clinical history, was invited to tell his own story in his own way and in his own time, a truly radical departure from being peremptorily dosed and discharged. Healy's clinical design provided a basic structure for treatment planning that has endured until today, incorporating the principles of psychological testing, collaborative diagnosis, and interdisciplinary treatment within the framework of a dynamic, developmental psychopathology.[8]

In the 1930's, child analysis and play therapy arrived in America and child psychotherapy became a teachable technique with a rich theoretical foundation.

Having approached the problems of individual psychotherapy, the child clinician began to look beyond the individual to his family, his social group, his educational environment, and his total culture. The need to work with parents, schools and communities became more apparent. In the decades that followed, there was, in consequence, a burgeoning of family, group and community therapy, behavior therapy, abreactive and hypnotic treatment, drug therapy, day care and residential treatment, and a variety of psychoeducational measures. This multidimensional therapeutic model, constructed, as Erikson put it, from inside out, took cognizance of the physical, the psychological, the familial, the social and the cultural factors that coalesce to make the child what he is, for better or for worse.

With the spectrum of diagnosis and treatment thus enlarged and enhanced, it was clear that child psychiatry had come a long way since 1859, when Crichton Browne [9] declared to the Royal Medical Society of Edinburgh that "the mental aberrations of infancy and childhood, excepting idiocy and imbecility, may be said to be yet uninvestigated, undescribed. The field is untrodden! The land unexplored!"

But the existence of more diagnoses and more therapies did not by any means guarantee that a particular diagnosis would automatically be correlated with an appropriate form of treatment. There was still an awkward gap between the two that required careful and close analysis if the matching was to be made more efficiently. The matchmakers themselves were not by any means exempt from difficulties of their own. As theoretical frames of reference became increasingly diverse, the interdisciplinary team began to experience problems of communication, with the result that the child sometimes fell between the uncoordinated efforts of these well-intentioned professionals. This particular difficulty has been eloquently described by no less an authority than Piaget [10]: "Imagine," he said at an interdisciplinary conference, "that some poor child has been studied by each of us for a long time and that we needed to coordinate our results. We would know his brain rhythm, his rate of physical growth, his conflicts with his family, his relation to his social environment, his capacity for problem solving, his verbal competence, his art productions, etc., but, and this is the tragedy of present circumstances, we would be incapable, without a common language, of achieving anything other than an enormous dossier. . . . Each specialist would continue to tell his own separate story in his own separate language without bringing about any real synthesis." In the clinic, this lack of coordination, based on the lack of communication, can insure a treatment failure even before the treatment has had a chance to begin. The implication is that the members of the clinical team must learn to live comfortably together and interchange clearly and regularly if the dossiers they compile are not to become monuments to failure.

This book is concerned with illuminating this "awkward gap" between diagnosis and treatment that can so very easily become a divisive chasm. Its purpose is to make the leap from diagnosis to treatment less mysterious and more a matter of everyday smooth clinical functioning. In order to carry out this purpose, it presents a microanalysis of the sequence of events stretching from one to the other side of the gap. A meaningful continuity between what has gone before and what is planned to come is firmly established so that the clinical procedure takes its logical place among the "lines of development" leading unbrokenly from the historical past to the diagnostic present and, when necessary, into the therapeutic future.

REFERENCES

1. J. Louise Despert. THE EMOTIONALLY DISTURBED CHILD—THEN AND NOW (New York: Robert Brunner, 1965).
2. Phillippe Aries. CENTURIES OF CHILDHOOD: A SOCIAL HISTORY OF FAMILY LIFE (New York: Alfred A. Knopf, 1962); translated by R. Baldick.
3. Leo Kanner. "Outline of the History of Child Psychiatry," in ESSAYS ON THE HISTORY OF MEDICINE, S. R. Kagen, Ed (New York: Froben Press, 1948).
4. Sigmund Freud. "A Phobia in a Five-year-old Boy," in COLLECTED PAPERS, Vol. III (London: Hogarth Press, 1948).
5. Jean M. G. Itard. THE WILD BOY OF AVEYRON (New York: Appleton-Century, 1932); translated by G. & M. Humphrey.

6. Leonard G. Guthrie. FUNCTIONAL NERVOUS DISORDERS IN CHILD-
   HOOD (London: Oxford University Press, 1907).
7. Richard Hunter & Ida Macalpine. THREE HUNDRED YEARS OF
   PSYCHIATRY (London: Oxford University Press, 1963) pp 1535-
   1860.
8. Lawson G. Lowrey. Psychiatry for Children: A Brief History
   of Developments, *American Journal of Psychiatry* 101(1944):
   375-388.
9. J. Crichton Browne. Psychical Diseases in Early Life, *Asylum
   Journal of Mental Science* 6(1860):284-320.
10. Jean Piaget. DISCUSSIONS ON CHILD DEVELOPMENT, Vol. IV, J. M.
    Tanner & B. Inhelder, Eds (New York: International Universi-
    ties Press, 1960) pp 5-6.

2

AN INTRODUCTION TO TREATMENT PLANNING

Wherefore I do conclude this part of moral knowledge, concerning the culture and regiment of the mind; wherein if any man, considering the parts thereof which I have enumerated, do judge that my labor is but to collect into an art or science that which hath been pretermitted by others, as matter of common sense and experience, he judgeth well.

Sir Francis Bacon (1605)

THE CONCEPT OF TREATMENT PLANNING

The sequence of diagnosis and treatment is a complex one. *It is to the process which takes place between the diagnostic formulation and the ultimate treatment recommendations that we have given the name of treatment planning.*

Diagnostic classification versus clinical assessment

In medical practice, diagnostic evaluations tend to favor the careful investigation of the patient's diseased or malfunctioning body parts and systems. The healthy, well-functioning ones are eliminated from further differential scrutiny once their lack of involvement in the pathological condition has been ascertained.

In psychiatry, and even more so in child psychiatry, the patient's areas of healthy functioning require as equally careful a differential assessment as do his areas of malfunctioning.

59

Evaluation in depth of the strengths and weaknesses of the child's family and extended environment is yet another indispensable dimension of a comprehensive diagnostic assessment. Only integration of the various facets of the child and his total life situation provides the matrix for a composite diagnostic appraisal suited to serve as a guideline for treatment planning.

Planning and the extended range of treatment

For the physically ill child, treatment planning consists of prescription of those specific measures likely to restore his health in the quickest and most effective way.

The child who displays signs of psychic disturbance is not necessarily sick in the same sense. Children suffering from reactive disorders or developmental deviations are examples of children who display symptoms that are not signs of illness in the strictly medical sense. They can be healthy responses to traumatic events, to overwhelming environmental stresses, or to temporary incongruities in the rate at which the child is developing in the physical, intellectual or emotional sphere.

Effective diagnosis and treatment planning therefore presupposes inclusion of developmental and adaptive considerations. Hence, the term *treatment* encompasses an extended range of curative, ameliorative and health-promoting procedures. They are aimed at supporting the child's potential for healthy development, accelerating the reversal of potentially pathological trends or states, and enhancing the constructive forces in his environment while combating or neutralizing the destructive, pathogenic ones. *In view of the complexity of the task, it is not surprising that treatment planning becomes an essential intermediary step between diagnosis and treatment in child psychiatry.*

Effective treatment planning requires the collaboration of various specialists such as child psychiatrists, pediatricians, neurologists, psychologists, social workers, educators, public health nurses and others whose contributions were instrumental in helping to formulate the diagnosis.

Having integrated his own findings with those of other child specialists, the treatment planner—that is, the person in that particular setting who carries primary responsibility for the case—can formulate one or more therapeutic approaches that take into account the whole child in his total environment and not just his psychopathological condition. Optimal planning will take into consideration the emotional climate of the child's milieu, the aspirations, assets and liabilities of his parents, and the demands imposed upon them by the size and constellation of their immediate family and extended environment.

Treatment planning may result in a number of treatment recommendations. Although he will probably favor some approaches over others, the planner, in discussing his recommendations with his patient and/or family, may find that their suggestions and choices alter his own views. This aspect of treatment planning can be therapeutic in itself because it allows the family to participate actively in the planning process and to play a role in decision making. Surprisingly, the therapeutic potentials of the family and its resources are often overlooked.

PRINCIPLES OF DIFFERENTIAL TREATMENT PLANNING

Diagnostic labels do not necessarily determine the most appropriate treatment intervention, although they do of course influence its selection. Other facets of the child's personality and existence require equal and at times even greater consideration. We can group these according to the child, his family, and his extended environment. Differential treatment planning requires the weighing of the relative importance and relevance of these various facets in the pathogenesis of the child's disorder.

The younger a child, the greater is his dependence upon his family or caretakers for day-to-day survival. Therapeutic planning for a young child will therefore require a different kind of parental participation and investment than planning for the older child and adolescent. Treatment of a young child is usually effective only if his parents can adjust better to his needs in their daily management of him. Planning must consider the parents' ability to modify their emotional attitudes and expectations regarding him.

Quite often a child becomes the target of frustrations and tensions within the family, when in reality these have little to do with him. Nevertheless, they indirectly affect his sense of security and well-being and may give rise to symptoms or behavioral disturbances. In such cases, treatment planning will focus less on rehabilitating the child and more on dealing with the pathogenic family group or parental coalition.

The older the child, the more the importance of his parents and family will shift in emphasis from the realm of physical care to that of emotional support, approval, judicious guidance, and discipline. Others, such as teachers and peers, become increasingly important to him. Because he is able to realize and express feelings about himself and others verbally, to understand them better, and because he has a great capacity to modify his behavior at will, he is from one standpoint more treatable than the younger child. At the same time, his keen awareness of his own feelings and the feelings of others, his anger and guilt, his need for independence and privacy, and his closeness to his peers may make him less accessible to therapeutic intervention. This is especially true if his family and teachers fix the responsibility for his misbehavior or malfunctioning entirely on him. In this case, treatment planning requires enlisting the cooperation of teachers, school counselors, youth officers, and others in order to create conditions favorable for the patient's treatment. It will also tax the skill and ingenuity of the planner to develop viable therapeutic recommendations with which all can agree enough to make cooperation or collaboration possible.

An alternative treatment plan becomes necessary when the initial plans (considered optimal) cannot be implemented because the patient, his parents or significant others, or external factors set obstacles in the path to the therapy recommended. In either case, the planner will need to spend time enlisting the cooperation of the family in supporting his recommendation. He may also have to seek the assistance of others to help overcome difficulties stemming from any pressing family needs and social exigencies. If, however, other ameliorative procedures that are more realistic in view of the circumstances can also be seriously considered, the planner must be open-minded, flexible and imaginative enough to adapt his recommendation to what child, family and community can manage best.

This does not mean that he "gives in" to the family, or shirks his professional responsibility against his better judgment. There are times, for example, when inpatient treatment or foster home placement is essential for the child's welfare. In such cases the planner cannot in good conscience give way to the patient's or family's displeasure and abide by their non-therapeutic alternatives. This kind of impasse is particularly apt to arise with severely disturbed, homicidal or suicidal children and adolescents.

Treatment planning for the less seriously disturbed adolescent depends in great measure upon the patient's willingness to cooperate. Maturational and developmental considerations are especially important in this age group, and treatment modalities have to take into account the natural striving for independence and emancipation from, as well as vestiges of dependence on, parental figures so characteristic of the teenager.

The child may need various combinations of therapeutic measures concomitantly or sequentially. Individual psychotherapy may not always be the most desirable or even the most appropriate mode of intervention. The planner may recommend other ameliorative, corrective and rehabilitative procedures, such as group or milieu therapy, behavior modification, chemotherapy, tutoring, special education or placement.

The treatment planner is dependent upon collaboration with other specialists for the formulation of a range of procedures, some of which do not fall within his special area of competence. He need not be defensive if he is not proficient in the management or supervision of all techniques of therapeutic intervention, but he should be knowledgeable enough about them to recognize their unique value for certain kinds of children and problems. He is easily put into a defensive position by medical colleagues, by educators, and by other child-care personnel if his therapeutic alternatives consist only of intensive psychotherapy, psychoanalysis, or treatment in a psychiatric residential setting, or if he has no therapeutic alternative to behavior modification. Unfortunately, systematic and convincing follow-up studies on children treated by one method rather than another, or left untreated, are lacking. Matching of symptoms or symptom clusters with treatment procedures is practiced by all clinicians, but the criteria upon which such matching is based are subjective insofar as they reflect the professional bias of the clinician.

When his recommendations arouse the patient's or the family's objections because they pose a threat to the family equilibrium, require financial sacrifices, create complicated transportation problems, interfere with the patient's daily routines, or for any other reason, the clinician may be tempted to modify his recommendations in ways more pleasing to his colleagues, the child, the parents, or others in the community. The line between flexible adaptation to reality and irresponsible acquiescence to "political" pressures is at times hard to draw, and even more difficult to hold.

Where a preschool child is concerned, his parents, pediatrician and nursery school teacher often cling to the conviction that the child will outgrow his difficulties spontaneously. Because we cannot predict with certainty a young child's future development, we may be inclined to "let things go."

For parents of a latency child who in the early school grades shows signs of an incipient neurotic learning inhibition, a change of teacher or school, extra tutoring, or strict enforcement of homework routines is often a far more palatable recommendation than psychotherapeutic intervention for him and themselves. Although there is ample clinical evidence that many of these children develop severe learning difficulties in time, the treatment planner, even though he is quite sure his patient has such a prognosis, may find himself up against much organized objection and may be sorely tempted to drop his recommendation for psychiatric treatment.

The rebellious, disturbed adolescent who suffers from a chronic character neurosis or acting-out personality disorder poses a different type of therapeutic problem. While his rehabilitation requires the concerted efforts of any number of persons involved in his daily life, their hostility toward him may be so pervasive that temporary removal from his home environment becomes necessary. Rather than make a strenuous effort to convince the patient and his family that drastic measures are needed, the planner may drop the case or agree to untherapeutic plans. Therapeutic treatment planning will often require a great deal of time-consuming exploration, investigation, and personal effort on the part of the clinician.

Unfortunately, certain diagnostic labels tend to discourage differential treatment planning altogether. Because we are presently lacking ameliorative procedures likely to improve significantly the condition of the autistic, brain-damaged or retarded child, treatment planning for such patients is apt to be unimaginative, often inappropriate, or worse—altogether absent.

Treatment recommendations mainly determined by resources that are easily accessible but are insufficiently equipped to deal with the problems of a particular disturbed child also tend to influence treatment planning adversely. Many facilities, both outpatient and residential, are so overloaded with children referred to them that what they can offer the patient is insufficient or even contraindicated.

With the rising demand for "treatment" for increasing numbers of children who are seriously disturbed and severely socioeconomically and culturally deprived, application of screening methods and triage will become more and more necessary. We suffer from a serious shortage of highly trained professional personnel and will continue to do so.

Treatment planning will improve as we are able to develop methods for screening and triage. These could lead to a better use of available personnel and treatment and make it possible to plan for and treat larger numbers of children more effectively.

Differential treatment planning consists of selecting, in order of priority, curative, corrective, ameliorative or palliative approaches to a child patient, his family, and, when needed, his extended environment. Such planning takes the fullest advantage of the available assets in the child, his family and his community.

3

THERAPEUTIC ASPECTS OF GOOD TREATMENT PLANNING (A SERENDIPITOUS EFFECT)

There are a number of truisms familiar to the clinician that he nevertheless overlooks in his day-to-day work. Because in some measure we all possess this capacity for turning a blind eye to the obvious, we are justified in repeating therapeutic axioms here that have been stated often before without much apparent effect. In saying them again, systematically and comprehensively, it is our hope that their cumulative influence may have greater impact than sporadic references in the literature, and that the therapist will pay more conscious attention to them. It is the overall aim of this report to make the latent process of treatment planning more manifest.

In this section, we would point out that often diagnosis is treatment and treatment remains essentially diagnostic to its very end. That this can be so is irrespective of the diagnostician's intentions. He may have very clear ideas in his planning as to when his part of the task, "diagnosis," ends and someone else's work, "treatment," begins. But the patient may confound his intentions and develop "prematurely" a profound therapeutic alliance and response. This may prove an embarrassment to the plan in that the official therapist may find himself coming in on an established and ongoing relationship. In this context, the diagnostic process can be regarded as accelerated treatment; there is an intensive uncovering process, sometimes amounting to abreaction, with little if any "working through" of the material with the help of a therapist. The rapid acquisition of sensitive psychological knowledge and the by-passing of defenses may have repercussions in later therapy with an increase in resistance. The patient may also experience and express disappointment at the loss of impetus and intensity that normally accompanies the transition from diagnosis to treatment. Direct questions and active probing may be re-placed by more passive techniques, depending on the style of the therapist.

The planner must constantly bear in mind that whatever one does for a patient—whether it is giving him an appoint-ment, listening to his complaints, evaluating him, or planning his treatment—is likely to improve his general contact with the world at large and bring about some improvement in his behavior or functioning.

The diagnostic process in psychological medicine is essentially therapeutic in a more direct way. In the cooperative patient it can be a creative period in life which allows him to develop a more comprehensive, unified and intelligible past and present, and even provide some outline for the future. It reviews his life for him and brings about meaningful connections between what he once was and what he is now. The use of projectives and projective interviewing may furnish him with insights or the beginnings of insights, may provoke needed catharsis when the "secrets" are near the surface. Treatment planning reas-sures the patient that his problem is still treatable and much of it lies inside himself, so that he is to some extent the master of his own fate. The family as a whole may have found out a number of things about themselves in relation to the patient: The problem is not his alone; they have means within them-selves for ameliorating and aggravating it; they had some re-sponsibility for generating it; and realignments and reconsid-erations are better than recriminations. If the family has been interviewed together they may have developed ideas on how to communicate therapeutically with one another. The parents may have identified with the therapist as a good parent and may have resolved to try out the new approach to their child. A certain amount of "meta-learning" goes on throughout the diagnostic and planning stage.

If this is in fact true that good treatment planning is serendipitous because it possesses a therapeutic aspect which is, for the most part, unintentional, then it should be possible to observe this helpfulness in practice.

A STUDY OF WAITING-LIST DROPOUTS

At a university psychiatric clinic for children and adolescents, a group of children and families had been placed on a treatment waiting list after having been taken through a diagnostic study. Analysis of the refusal rate (30 per cent) on the part of waiting-list candidates revealed a wide variety of causes. There were two main groups: those who had become worse (28 per cent); and those who had become better plus those who had remained the same (72 per cent).

Those who became worse

Of this group, some (the majority) were still waiting for treatment, constantly inquiring and increasingly resigned or resentful. A small number had taken themselves off to other clinics or private practitioners. The worsening of their condition was attributed variously to:

> A—Extraneous factors, such as divorce, separation, illness in the family, deterioration in economic circumstances, intervened.
>
> B—The nature of the illness was deteriorating by definition, since the factors inside the child behaved like a malignant growth.
>
> C—Lack of guidance and treatment was mainly responsible.
>
> D—No cause could be conceived for the worsening.
>
> E—The diagnostic and planning processes were the causal

factors: "just stirred up things in our family"; "he just took advantage of the things you people said blaming us and he simply played up; it gave him an excuse for being mean to us; if we told him to mind he said he'd report us to you"; "he's never been the same kid since all this happened; he puts on airs; his dad and I think it's gone to his head; he's too important now, that's what he is."

Factor E was attributed as the cause of the worsening in only 3 cases of the 25 in this group.

Those who become better or remained the same

Of this group, some were still on the waiting list but the majority had taken themselves off the list. The bettering of their condition was attributed to various factors:

A—Intervening extraneous factors, such as a change of schools, joining the scouts, or undergoing religious confirmation, acted as a boost.

B—The nature of the illness by definition made it susceptible to remission or recovery: "It was just a stage"; "he's grown out of it"; "his sister went through the same thing when she was his age."

C—Some good advice had been obtained from neighbors, relatives, clergyman or pediatrician, and it had helped.

D—No reason for the bettering could be given; these things just happen.

E—The diagnostic and planning processes were mainly responsible: "I found talking about the problem very helpful; I had never talked to anyone before about it. I thought I'd feel ashamed but it wasn't like that at all, they never criticized at all—they just listened nicely"; "for the first time we really understood what it was all about, it seemed so clear"; "all his complaints disappeared after you tested him and they haven't come back—

the whole family has felt better since we all talked to you even though you really didn't do anything for her as you might say"; "it was understanding everything that counted, from the time he was born. It all made sense, and I knew then what I had been doing all the time. It was a good feeling to understand—I had been so confused before."

A small number of those in the second group presented a "flight into health" and expressed some anxiety about the dangers involved in treatment. Perhaps some were saying what they thought we wanted to hear. Others of this group had clearly learned to live more comfortably with their symptoms and expressed a higher level of frustration tolerance. A very small number from both groups felt that the act of waiting had broken the "spell" or the "rhythm" and they could not muster up enough energy, time, money or interest to begin what they viewed as the interminable process of treatment.

Factor E was assigned as the cause of the bettering by an appreciable number in the second group, 17 out of 35.

WAITING-LIST DEFECTORS

Levitt [1] has pointed out that it was customary in the past to ascribe treatment refusals to "resistance," but that in quite a few cases refusal probably represented inadequate communication by clinic personnel with the family. He felt it important to distinguish between those who defected while waiting for treatment and those who dropped out during treatment.

Defections from a treatment waiting list could be due to many factors some of which might serve to differentiate defectors' families from the families of those who accepted treatment.[2] Among factors to be considered are severity of disturbance, distance from the clinic, time on the waiting list, and improvement. According to Magder and Wherry,[3] the defector is significantly a Protestant child (as contrasted with more accepting Roman Catholics and Jews), who lives further from the clinic and has been waiting for a shorter period than the one who remains. In addition, his condition is less serious and his improvement while on the waiting list more frequent. One-third of the parents interviewed in this particular study said they were no longer interested in receiving help, the most common reason being "significant improvement" in the child. It may well be that some of these "improvements" are manifestations of resistance, second thoughts on the part of poorly motivated parents who have waited too long, or a denial of the seriousness of the presenting complaint. But the authors also argue that in some cases the improvement may be genuine and a valid reason for defection. Resistance may generate improvement or improvement may bring on resistance.

Treatment waiting-list improvements may also occur because the family approached the clinic during a temporary crisis which was subsiding or because a curative process was initiated by the family's recognition of its need for help.[4]

These various considerations imply that treatment planners need to be aware of the influence of waiting on the child and his family and of the significant effect that the changes which occur may make on their treatment plan. It is therefore important to keep in close touch with the waiting families and in some cases to institute transitional therapies to tide them over a difficult period.

REFERENCES

1. E. E. Levitt. Parents' Reasons for Defection from Treatment at a Child Guidance Clinic, *Mental Hygiene* 42(1958):521-524.
2. A. Inman. Attrition in Child Guidance: A Telephone Follow-up Study, *Smith College Studies in Social Work* 24(1956):34-73.
3. D. Magder & J. S. Wherry. Defection from a Treatment Waiting List in a Child Psychiatric Clinic, *Journal of the American Academy of Child Psychiatry* 5(1966):706-720.
4. J. Hood-Williams. The Results of Psychotherapy with Children, *Journal of Consulting Psychology* 24(1960):84-88.

4

ASSESSMENT OF THERAPEUTIC POTENTIAL

The variety of factors entering into the assessment of therapeutic potential seems nearly limitless and depends to a significant degree upon the ability of the clinician to conceptualize them. Some factors are clear-cut, self-evident and easily recognized by all involved in the therapeutic planning. Many, however, are not well articulated, are murky and at times completely outside awareness. Assessment factors are sought out, recorded and thought through during the diagnostic process, but it is during the crucial phase between diagnosis and treatment that all factors identified must be brought together in a practical harmony for realistic treatment planning and implementation.

Although they may be organized in several ways, there seem to be four major areas for consideration:

1. The clinician or team
2. The child
3. The family
4. The community

1. THE CLINICIAN OR TEAM

The "diagnostic mind" itself is composed of many variables. The past personal history, professional training, cultural experience, geographic locations, age and sex of the clinician or members of the team all exert an influence in the appraisal of therapeutic potential. The clinical facts of a given case are processed and an assessment is made. Ideally this would reflect the current "state of the patient" as ascertained by the collective clerical knowledge and experience of the group. In practice, however, the need to get something done frequently compels the clinicians to bring their assessment to a premature closure, thus limiting the exploration of new and imaginative approaches. Once a diagnosis is reached, attitudes are apt to consolidate around it and generate optimistic or pessimistic expectations that block a more realistic evaluation of the therapeutic potential. For example, if a diagnosis of maternal deprivation is made, the clinician may assess the therapeutic potential as nil, based on his own experience and on published reports. As a consequence, he may overrate the extent of the deprivation and underrate the resilience of the child, or the effect of devoted and capable surrogates. The reverse is true when, because of his optimism in spite of clinical evidence, he considers the deprived child to be treatable and spends an inordinate amount of clinical time attempting to justify his hunch.

Treatability and therapeutic potential are often linked with the individual clinician's conception of the therapeutic goal. If this involves a major personality change in the child and his parents, and their capacity for change does not measure up to requirements, the case may then be considered untreatable. Once the therapeutic potential is assessed, the goal will, in a sense, be set. If the child can be helped only a little, he is treatable to that degree. The extent to which the style, values and socioeconomic class of the child and his family approximate those of the clinician may determine his appraisal of their treatability and the goals he has set for them. If they are set too high, he may overlook the potential for making life a little more tolerable or less symptomatic without inducing major characterological shifts. An important clinical axiom in this context is treatment planning—*no* child should be considered untreatable in the present state of our knowledge. Only after various treatments or interventions have been at- tempted without success may a child be considered untreatable by the methods available. In part, the fact that a child is regarded as unreachable may be the clinician's problem, and it is an important task for him to make himself aware of these possible biases by ongoing self-scrutiny and vigilance.

2. THE CHILD

Focusing on the assessment of elements within the child, the following may be considered:

1—degree of CNS or physical impairment
2—areas of healthy function
3—capacity for relating to others
4—capacity for tolerance of anxiety
5—capacity for conceptualization and communication
6—developmental phase
7—personality structure (drive, conscience, ego)
8—frustration tolerance
9—duration of the problem
10—severity of the disorder
11—"psychological mindedness"
12—proportion of reactive to intrapsychic elements
13—degree of secondary gain
14—proneness to regression

These broad categories are matched to the child during the diagnostic process in varying intensities and combinations. The ratio of "good" to "bad" potential must be considered in making an overall assessment. A child with a severe chronic characterological disorder but with an excellent capacity for conceptualization, psychological mindedness, and object relations might be judged to have a good therapeutic potential despite his chronic severe problem. On the other hand, a child with a relatively mild disorder but with a high degree of secondary gain, little capacity for communication, and a low tolerance for frustration might be considered to have less therapeutic potential. Moreover, these elements must be viewed in relation to the passage of time. Passage from latency to adolescence, for example, may shift the balance of factors so that the assessment of potential will shift from low to high or vice versa. Furthermore, a new capacity for introspection can radically alter the assessment even though none of the other variables have changed.

3. THE FAMILY

These listed elements cannot be considered in isolation, but must be integrated with the assessment of the child in the family and of the family as a unit, for example:

1—The nature of the family as a unit (stable, cohesive, divisive, close, distant)

2—Family capacity for cooperation with treatment plans

3—Psychological mindedness of members of the family

4—The capacity for communication between family members

5—The degree of mental health or ill health of the family as a unit or in terms of the individual members

6—The role of the child's disorder in the psychic economy of the family (secondary gain, or family misuse of the child's disorder)

7—The relationship of the family to the community (distant, isolated, involved)

8—The subcultural values dominant on the family

It goes without saying that the family which rates high in cooperation, stability, solidarity and emotional healthiness will also be highly rated on its therapeutic potential, however they might be involved in the treatment of the child. Or, despite these assets, they might be so isolated from the community that a therapeutic plan involving the neighborhood could be jeopardized, as for instance when a local remedial resource or activity program is included. A child who himself is judged to have good therapeutic potential might receive a low overall rating if his family is found to be pessimistic, uncooperative, psychologically dependent on the child's illness and, directly or obliquely, ready to sabotage the plan. It is left to the clinical judgment of the planning team to determine whether the child's assets are sufficient to compensate for the family's liabilities.

The extended family—grandparents, aunts, uncles and cousins—must also be mentioned, since they can often supplement, implement or undermine the therapeutic management. Changing life styles in the United States, with its increasing residential and social mobility, coupled with the nuclear family's independence from the extended family group, have loaded the full burden of child rearing on the parents, who frequently receive little emotional support from other adults. Similarly, the children are bereft of significant adults who can step in and take over if one or the other parent is faltering. Clinicians in this country have become so accustomed to working only with the nuclear family, especially in the middle classes, that they are likely to overlook the therapeutic possibilities latent in the extended family.

In the case of the child in an institution, members of the staff become the family surrogates and the same factors already enumerated would have to be assessed for them, but the quality of institutional care, the size of the facility, and the nature of the patient population would contribute another important dimension in assessment of the therapeutic potential.

4. THE COMMUNITY

The ambient community represents the fourth but not least important dimension in the evaluation. In this respect, the planner needs to consider

1—the attitude of the school personnel and their investment in the child
2—the peer relationships and attitudes
3—the juvenile court and its personnel, where relevant
4—geographic (urban-suburban-rural) and economic factors
5—cultural, social, recreational, and religious opportunities and practices
6—the range of helping facilities available (clinics, agencies, therapeutic camps, big brother groups)

Here the paradox of the "poor rich" and the "rich poor" emerges. It is not sufficient for facilities to be available in a community—the clinics must know about them in terms of their advantages and disadvantages, and the families referred must be in a position to use them. The most advantageously placed community will be of relatively little help if the family is disorganized and disinterested, or where an impulse-ridden child is too far out of control to be manageable at the facilities provided. On the other hand, a child with internal disorder who has high intelligence, good ego strength, and a strong desire to change can transcend or bypass a disadvantaged community with few funds or facilities. An impoverished locale, however, tends to "specialize" in acting-out problems so that its lack of resources is acutely highlighted.

In assessing the therapeutic potential of a particular child patient, it has seemed logical to move from the child, through the family, to the environment. This does not by any means represent a ranking order of importance, since these factors will vary with the case, and will vary in the same case at different stages of development. For example, as the child improves internally, external factors assume greater importance and vice versa. Again, children with certain types of disorders are more accessible to certain types of therapy. The assessment might prove favorable for behavior modification but unfavorable for individual psychotherapy—or more favorable for environmental change or for family therapy than for either of the first two therapies.

The assessment of therapeutic potential is therefore best used when it takes into account both internal and external environments of the child, both strengths and weaknesses, both patient and therapist, keeping well in the forefront what happens in "the other 23 hours," when the community is called upon to exercise its collective helpfulness. It is poorly used if used for the purpose of deciding which children will receive therapeutic intervention and which children will be passed by or assigned to a more-or-less permanent waiting list.

5

DYNAMICS OF SMALL-GROUP PLANNING

In child psychiatry, the development of a treatment plan for a disturbed child and his family frequently requires small-group collaboration. The potential value of a treatment plan designed by a group depends as much on the quality of team collaboration as on the diagnostic picture and treatment resources available. Those who coordinate the efforts of treatment-planning teams must constantly consider the dynamics of small-group interaction, which can profoundly influence the outcome of team deliberations.

DIFFERENT TEAM ORGANIZATIONS

In 1950 Alexander Bavelas [1] examined the decision-making activities of small groups confronted with a problem. He describes two types of groups—the circle group and the star group. It is not at all difficult to find correlates for these groups among therapeutic teams. In the circle group (or team), each member talks freely to other members of the circle and nothing in the structure of the group favors one person over another as leader. This would correspond to a free-wheeling democratic organization. In the star group (or team), on the other hand, one person is definitely in a key position; he may communicate freely with all the other members but they generally communicate with each other only through him. This represents a more autocratic setup.

The members of the circle team tended on the whole to be rather unsystematic in reaching decisions, and no one emerged consistently as a leader. Each member was openly critical of team efficiency but apparently enjoyed the conference and, what was more important, made no effort to sabotage it. The members of the star team had a rather high opinion of their organization, but, except for their leader, a rather low opinion of themselves. They felt unimportant and became increasingly dissatisfied as they handled more and more problems with less and less participation. There were quite a few cases of conscious and unconscious sabotage. Decision-making activities were concluded more rapidly, but morale was by no means as high as it was in the circle team. Under crisis conditions, when unusual pressure was brought to bear on the work of the teams, the circle team came into its own, revealing an unusual ability to adapt to the demands of the crisis.

Bavelas concluded that no form of team organization is ideal for all circumstances. Running an emergency clinic might entail quite different forms of team organization from those suitable for the typical diagnostic clinic.

Illustration No. 1: The director of the clinic, a staff psychologist and a junior staff social worker participated in a treatment-planning conference. After each had presented his point of view, the director made the following statement: "Well, in summing up, I would say he's suffering from a character disorder with the usual history going back to disturbances in very early life. Since there is a report of infantile colic, I would very much doubt that this child ever had a normal phase of development. For this reason, I would question Barry's conclusion that there is an intense oedipal conflict, since there is very little evidence to indicate that he ever got beyond the preoedipal stage of development. Clancy has described the mother in favorable terms but if, as I suspect, this is a case of a primary behavior disorder, this mother would be, by definition if nothing else, a somewhat rejecting person. It would seem to me that she is one of those people who can turn on feelings for another adult but is unable to respond adequately with children. Any questions? None? Well let's get on with the next case then."

Illustration No. 2: A treatment-planning session is taking place between the resident, the senior psychiatric social worker and the chief psychologist, who is speaking: "I suppose we should try and get some conclusions; what's your opinion, Bob?" Bob replies: "I'm not so sure what to think. I was quite influenced by Margaret's remark that she felt very positive about working with the parents. I can't say I felt so positive about the prospect of working with the kid, but I'm willing to have a try." Margaret comments: "Don't rely too much on what I said. I've not had too much experience with this sort of case, but there was something about the way in which the parents dealt with one another's questions that made me very hopeful. Why don't we have a trial run, telling the family about our doubts, and see how it works out? It may work very well and surprise us all." Susan has this to say: "Well, the projectives would be on your side because they indicate a lot of strength in the child. I feel good about these projectives and if Bob isn't anxious to treat Tommy, I would volunteer since I have open time. It's up to you, Bob." Bob replies: "No, I think I'll take him on and if I get into any difficulties, I'll check with you again about those projectives." Margaret sums up: "Well, it seems we've reached agreement, so let's plan our conference with the family."

TEAM COMMUNICATION

In a surprising number of cases the team functions remarkably well, with a minimum of friction. The members appear to communicate during and after the diagnostic period in a way that allows enough knowledge to be exchanged so that decision-making can proceed. The reason it works most of the time is not easy to understand unless one assumes that accurate communication is not absolutely necessary and that it is quite possible to get along on approximations for the purpose of reaching a treatment plan.

A closer analysis of the team process makes it fairly obvious that what takes place is nearly always *a relative failure in communication followed by operation of a self-corrective mechanism in response to the failure.* As the team deliberates, with a variable admixture of comfort and discomfort, communications are interrupted as interpretations or clarifications are found to drift too far afield from the team's main line of thinking. The incidence of interruptions is the best evidence that although things may tend to go "off beam" from time to time, there is a built-in tendency to bring them back into line. The team deliberations thus develop in the form of a spiral rather than a line. The more spiral it is, the longer the team discussion tends to last before arriving at conclusions.

SOME GOLDEN RULES OF TEAM DELIBERATION

Certain rules regarding the communication process can be formulated:

1. It should be taken for granted that nothing any member of the team says can be completely communicated to the others in the exact sense in which it was meant. Even as the speaker listens to himself, he is often compelled to recognize that what he is saying in fact is not precisely what he intends to say.

2. Often the only way to offset the built-in distortion that results from communicating abstract data is a series of reciprocal interruptions by the team members. By these interruptions the speakers can adjust themselves to varying degrees of acceptance of their ideas and modulate their thinking along the general lines followed by the team.

3. From time to time, communication among team members fails grossly, as it does even in the best-regulated clinics. What is needed is an understand-

ing of the well-known phenomenon of countertransference—its influence on the clinician's deductions
and interpretations concerning the patient, and the
resultant distortion of his receptiveness to communications within the team. The awareness of this phenomenon makes it possible for someone to take
cognizance of the failure, make it evident, and provide some insight toward really effective communication.

Application of these rules in turn allows for increasing self-
perception on the part of the member who interferes, either
unconsciously or deliberately, with the mutual understanding
and consensus of the group. It does not and should not entail
the overt exploration of feelings and fantasies within the team
environment, since this would soon verge on group therapy, a
process different in both intent and practice from that of team
interaction. But it does involve the use of mutual insight into
the process of team functioning in the service of harmonious
team relationships. The team should strive to create an emotional climate that would allow for the comfortable expression
of those factors within each individual that might impede their
functioning as a team. At certain critical moments in team
deliberation, the sharing of such insights can bring about
striking changes in the attitude of the individual member
which allows the team to better its treatment planning for
the patient.

HOMOGENEOUS AND HETEROGENEOUS TEAMS

In the traditional child-guidance clinic setting, the treatment-
planning team usually consists of a small group. Its members
have worked together over a period of time, shared the same
goals, and drawn upon a common body of theory and technique.
The relative homogeneity of such a team carries with it both
advantages and disadvantages.

On the one hand, the commonality of assumptions and approaches can make possible the economical, consistent and sophisticated management of a variety of clinical situations. Mutual familiarity makes it unnecessary for the psychiatrist, the social worker, and the psychologist to define each other's roles and areas of expertise each time they meet to plan the treatment of a child and his family. They can begin at once to consider the problems of the case with a fair expectation of success in understanding and facilitating each other's contributions. A high degree of effectiveness in planning is therefore possible, often with a minimum of misunderstanding and friction.

On the other hand, the same homogeneity of orientation can gradually lead a team into narrowing its theoretical perspective and toward an increasingly rigid ritualization of procedure. An interested stranger sitting in on such a planning group might in such a situation be able to raise important questions which the forces of habit and conformity push aside during team deliberations that pursue only a familiar course. The usual team patterns of thought and action may prevail primarily because they are accepted operating procedure rather than because they are appropriate to features of a specific case or to the community situation within which the child must be treated.

The treatment-planning team, which consists of members of very different backgrounds, knowledge and experience, is much less likely to overlook important questions or succumb to outmoded planning rituals. By the same token, a more heterogeneous team whose members do not share the same attitudes and approaches toward the problems of treatment planning can also be more open to misunderstanding and destructive conflict. Until these differences are recognized and respected by the team members, overt or covert friction is inevitable and can lead to both inadvertent and willful failures of cooperation in treatment planning.

The problems of both homogeneous and heterogeneous teamwork become evident in one especially sensitive and increasingly common situation: For purposes of treatment planning the diagnostic team is temporarily expanded to include workers from collaborating community agencies. These visitors often strongly identify with their clients and are unfamiliar with the routine use of psychodynamic formulation as a guide to optimal intervention.

Illustration: A black neighborhood aide in a ghetto community is invited to participate in the treatment-planning conference for a multiproblem family with whom she has been involved. During presentation of the diagnostic findings, a white clinic social worker stresses the mother's strong masochistic tendencies. She feels they will limit the degree to which this mother will allow herself to better the living conditions of her family. The neighborhood aide interrupts and points out with considerable feeling that she and the mother have tried repeatedly but have been unable to obtain better housing because it is not available to low-income black families in the area. The clinic social worker, somewhat annoyed at this interruption of her dynamic formulation, casually acknowledges the aide's remark but goes on to stress that the mother would certainly undermine any arrangements for a better apartment because of her masochism. The neighborhood worker says nothing more but thinks bitterly to herself that she is dealing with a racist social worker in a racist clinic. She resolves to disregard clinic recommendations in her future dealings with the family and to discourage the mother from returning to the clinic.

Both the neighborhood aide and the clinic social worker have made valuable comments during the conference, but they have failed to comprehend each other and thereby have lost the opportunity for cooperation in helping the family. Since the neighborhood worker has a strong positive relationship with the mother, she will effectively undermine all clinic efforts to engage the family and thereafter will herself avoid turning to professional staff of the clinic for help. Thus the failure in communication and collaboration carries a cost far beyond a breakdown in the treatment of one family.

THE ROLE OF THE LEADER

A sensitive and tactful team leader might have averted this costly failure in communication. Throughout the process of team deliberation the effective leader remains sensitive to the background, values, feelings and biases of his fellow team members, resonating both to overt and covert communications within the group. This sensitivity can become especially important in heterogeneous planning teams, where the risks of misunderstanding and divisiveness are at their height, as in the foregoing illustration. An alert leader might have rephrased the clinic social worker's statement about the mother's masochism, stressing the adaptive aspects of the mother's willingness to continue her struggle against great odds, both external and internal, and emphasizing the crucial and difficult role of the neighborhood aide in helping this mother to change existing family patterns when such formidable obstacles lie in her way. The aide could then begin to view the clinic staff as empathic and just as appreciative of "reality" problems as of psychological disability. She would see it as able to help her maximize the effectiveness of her own efforts through psychological understanding. At the same time the leader could help the clinic social worker see that the aide is in a uniquely favorable position to deal with masochistic tendencies which might otherwise undermine all work with the family, especially if the treatment recommendations for this mother must be confined to a traditional casework approach.

Much depends not only on the tolerance and timing of the leader, but also on his open-mindedness, on his interest, and on his enthusiasm and capacity for remaining curious about the case. A good leader looks upon each member of the planning team as a resource person with special interests and skills. If his idea of a successful planning session is too rigid and narrow, and if he tries to carry it through to the end without allowing for the emergence of diverse contributions by the team members in the normal process of group deliberation, he may feel that he has conducted a very successful session, whereas in reality only a small fraction of the inherent possibilities may have been considered.

A certain amount of noncommittal floundering is characteristic and necessary in the early part of a planning session. Indeed it may be important for the leader to keep the members from committing themselves too early to a line of action (and then sticking with it in order not to lose face). Such premature commitment has the additional unwanted effect of influencing others before they are ready to conclude deliberation. Or the free-floating process may be carried too far, so that the session becomes unduly diffuse and even anxiety-provoking.

As child mental health workers become more involved with other professionals and concerned laymen in the community, the opportunities for creative planning increase, but the necessary teamwork becomes more complex and difficult. The team leader of today not only must maintain a nondogmatic atmosphere for flexible planning with the staff within the mental health clinic, but must also work to achieve clear and productive dialogue between members of more heterogeneous planning teams both within and beyond the clinic. He must be a living example of Lao-Tze's great paradox that the greatest leader is he who seems to follow.

THE EMERGENCE OF THE COORDINATOR

When the essential aspects of the treatment plan have been appropriately identified by the planners, the next task is to identify the person who is to make sure that immediate and long-range goals will continue to be seen in context; that resources, services and personnel will be coordinated; that methods will be clarified and understood; and that implementation will be marked by flexibility, readiness to modify, and responsiveness to new situations and developments as they emerge. This person is designated the coordinator of the treatment plan.

The designation of such an agent offers a device to insure continuity of care for the patient, to achieve optimal and appropriate utilization of resources, to see that the patient does not get "lost" when changes in therapeutic plan or locale are made, that he does not get hung up on long waiting lists when he needs care at once, or that he does not get stuck at one point in his therapeutic program (in a hospital or children's center, for instance) although succeeding steps of care are appropriate and urgent.

As assignments are made, it is important that the key professionals in the concrete planning phase be held responsible for implementing major areas of the treatment plan. As others are brought in later, or as shifts in therapeutic emphasis occur, the new resources and personnel need to be clued in to the dynamics involved and to the reasons for shifts in the context of the overall therapeutic goal and plan.

Although the principles of coordination hold for all therapeutic plans, the task of coordination becomes more complicated as other resources in the community must be tapped to implement a projected treatment plan for a child and his family. The appropriate professional choice for coordinator—whether it be the psychiatrist, the psychiatric social worker, the psychiatric nurse or any appropriate mental health worker —depends on that person's interprofessional skills, his understanding of the therapeutic program, and his specific talents in his special area of training. In any case, it is the responsibility of the treatment planner to see that a coordinator is designated. As therapeutic plans shift, the coordinator may be replaced but it is a *sine qua non* that there be one.

As the emotional disturbance in the child and his family

goes through periods of exacerbation or remission, the treatment plan and services may call for a shift in locale—for example, in the case of the child who may need a period of hospitalization, or who needs day hospital or outpatient treatment after a period of hospitalization. But the coordinator's responsibility to the child and the family remains constant. At some point it might be better for the child to change his therapist, in order to have one who is attached to his treatment setting. In such a case the current therapist insures a continuum of responsibility by meeting with the new therapist and sending him the clinical data and the details of the therapeutic plan as it has been working to date. This kind of qualitative exchange between therapists demonstrates responsibility to the patient at its best. It is the responsibility of the coordinator (whether or not he is also the therapist) to see that the exchange takes place, insuring his child patient a clinical bridge to the next step in care.

Another example relates to those instances where a child returns to a former psychiatric service or agency, whether for more or less intensive care or for supportive follow-up. In such instances, the coordinator will see that the child is returned to the helping professional who has known him and whom he has known.

Simply to make a referral or to send a child and/or his family to another resource courts disaster for the patient. It is in such instances that a patient too frequently gets lost between agencies and becomes the responsibility of no one. Much good care previously given the patient can come to naught in such situations, which only add the traumatic effects of discontinuity of care to the patient and waste precious time and money.

For the achievement of these tasks, the projected treatment plan must be clear as to its purpose and goal; must specify appropriate and economical use of resources; and must utilize available personnel in a manner that is pertinent, creative and unwasteful.

Typically, the coordinator will face manpower shortages, inadequately trained personnel, trained workers being used in inappropriate ways, or untrained persons expected to do the job of a trained person. He should be alert to the need for new patterns of use of trained manpower and for new types of helping and supportive personnel.

On the other hand, there will be resources and agencies eager to work out ways for fruitful collaboration, as well as agencies that wish to confine themselves to their own orbit and remain outside the total program for a child. Rigid departmental structures not infrequently pose for a coordinator the same type of problem. Duplication of resources will be noted as implementation is sought. Some existing services (new or ancient and honorable) will be found grossly inadequate, poor in quality, and pedestrian. In these areas the planner is in the position of fact-finder who is identifying major and chronic community needs. These shortcomings should be brought to the attention of those in the community who have the influence or power to remedy them. He should be ready to interpret, document and educate in behalf of the children he wishes to help.

REFERENCE

1. Alexander Bavelas. "Communications Patterns in Task-Oriented Groups," in THE POLICY SCIENCES, D. Lerner & H. D. Lasswell, Eds (Stanford, Calif.: Stanford University Press, 1951).

6

TREATMENT PLANNING AND THE COMMUNITY

The following custom seems to be the wisest of their [Babylonians] institutions next to the one lately praised. They have no physicians, but when a man is ill, they lay him in the public square, and the passers-by come up to him, and if they have ever had his disease themselves or have known anyone who has suffered from it, they give him advice, recommending him to do whatever they found good in their own case, or in the case known to them; and no one is allowed to pass the sick man in silence without asking him what his ailment is.

Herodotus (484-425 B.C.)

THE CONCEPT: A NETWORK OF THERAPEUTIC RESOURCES

What happens in the other 23 hours of a patient's life when he is not involved in a formal treatment situation with a psychotherapist is becoming increasingly important even to the psychotherapist. The "echosphere" of a patient is made up of objects, human and nonhuman, animate and inanimate, any of which may serve a pathogenic or therapeutic purpose. Some of these have transient importance and some transitional, to be used when needed. There are a few, however, which represent the continuous and permanent elements in the patient's life. Their influence stretches across his days and gives meaning to his activities—without them he could experience loneliness and emptiness. None of these elements, whether temporary or permanent, exhibit as much emotional steadiness as the therapist. Even at their most therapeutic, they may be singularly devoid of insight. Since the diagnostic process is often concerned with linking a disturbance to a disturbing influence, the clinician dealing with a disturbed child is more likely to perceive hate emanating from the network of objects than love. It is well to remember, however, that an environment labeled pathogenic can also be full of loyalty, devotion and concern. In the general condemnation, these qualities tend to be overlooked.

The balance of "good" and "bad" in the total environment is as much in flux as the balance of "good" and "bad" within the patient. There may be times when the same environment is "not so bad" or "not so good," and the one opposite may be directly or indirectly related to the other. There is a primary network composed of the family, and beyond this a secondary network of influential others. The two networks can help us understand emotional disturbance as a social or interpersonal process as well as an intrapsychic one. The network is the frame of reference for the behavior of the patient, whether that behavior be expressed manifestly, symbolically, symptomatically, somatically or verbally. Moreover, the network has fundamental significance in the causation of emotional illness, but it can be effective in achieving cure or impeding it. A change in any component part of the network has repercussions throughout. It is in a state of dynamic equilibrium, and the patient's disturbance may affect this equilibrium at two points: one at the onset of the disturbance and the other at its cessation.

It is important for the clinician to map the network for his patient in terms of its therapeutic and nontherapeutic and/or pathogenic elements. He has then to mobilize as much that is therapeutic in the environment as is available, always bearing in mind that nonprofessional therapy is at best unreliable, unsteady, ambivalent and reversible. He must try to work with it but not depend on it. It can disrupt ongoing therapy, compete with it, or stimulate therapeutic changes that may leave the therapist pleasantly surprised. Every patient has one or more fairy godmothers in the offing with magical remedies to match anything that can be offered by the official therapist. Their powers often pass unnoticed, while credit is taken by the therapist unless treatment takes a turn for the worse, whereupon he is quickly able to unearth a witch.

The primary network is less able to function therapeutically than the secondary network because the family is more likely to be caught up inextricably in bad interactions. The family members, with the best conscious will, can and often do sabotage their own therapeutic efforts. In the secondary network of friends, relatives, teachers, tree houses and teddy bears the benign efforts may predominate in a less contaminated way.

The clinician's causal beliefs determine to what extent the "echosphere" is virtually neglected or is rendered significant in the treatment process. His focus may be almost exclusively on the intrapsychic, dyadic or triadic structures and on the historic past. To that extent, the interpersonal, the familial, the extrafamilial and the existential will recede into insignificance unless their pathogenicity is of such proportions as constantly to undermine the therapist's work. Similarly, the clinician's concept of treatment will govern the degree to which the "echosphere" is mobilized generally in the service of helpfulness. If he is wedded to a medical model and is certain that the cure resides exclusively in the person of the "doctor," his perception of the environment will not be in terms of varieties of benign forces manifestly or latently available to his patient.

In this context, emotional illness emerges as a social, interpersonal process. By the same token therapeutic help is a function of a multipersonal network of interaction. This network should always be the framework for diagnosis, treatment and prognosis even when an approach to all the elements of the network simultaneously is impractical. Psychosocial analysis of the network can furnish a key to the unconscious processes in three areas: to the personal, repressed unconscious of psychoanalysis; to the unconscious, interpersonal interactions, the "social unconscious"; and to the existing ills of society as a whole and thus to the unconscious origins of much human behavior.

The wise clinician counts all the blessings of the total environment and constantly perceives the interpersonal and impersonal network as a vast, largely untapped serendipitous pool of helpfulness in his treatment planning and treatment.

PLANNING WITH COMMUNITY RESOURCES

If you will tell me why the fen
appears impassible, I then
will tell you why I think that I
can get across it if I try *

Differential treatment planning leads by different labyrinthine paths out of the process of differential diagnosis. The solutions to problems posed by differential diagnosis are projected into the physical space of the community and the form given to the treatment plan must be a fair representation of the shape or form taken by the problems posed by the child and family.

Unfortunately this shape tends to be distorted by the community's apparent inability to provide the necessary resources. Differential treatment planning then involves an assessment (or diagnosis) of the actual resources of the community. This diagnostic process may be as complex as the procedure by which the child's emotional and mental state is evaluated and the diagnosis must be as accurate, if the most appropriate plan is to be made from the stuff of which any particular community is made.

* "I May, I Might, I Must," in THE COMPLETE POEMS OF MARIANNE MOORE (New York: Macmillan, 1967).

Attitudes toward the use of community resources should reflect a balance between positive anticipation and the ability to recognize the flat unavailability of certain forms of treatment. The treatment planner must see the community from inside, not from above looking down, or from outside looking in. The child psychiatrist and other planners are most usefully a part of the scene they survey. They gain by their membership in a number of different communities what they lose in objectivity. It is this actual participation in the life of any community which brings its hidden resources to light at the same time that certain of its vaunted resources are tried and found wanting.

As members of the community, the planners are limited by being of their particular time and place, but they know the geography. Community has been defined as *joint ownership, identity of character,* and *fellowship* **—optimistic definitions of a vantage point from which the treatment planner can approach his task in using community resources.

The family's relationship to the various communities in which its members live colors their relationship to the psychiatric community with which they come in contact during the planning process. In fact, the strength of their feelings often determines, or overdetermines, the acceptability of the plan.

The affective content of the interviews between planners and parents provides the therapeutic thrust for the parental involvement in the planning process. This is particularly important in communities where all planning is suspect. As the various institutions and agencies are discussed, the planners' acceptance of the feelings engendered becomes the basis for trust, and, in turn, the precursor of the therapeutic process.

In many communities in which planners share the families'

** THE CONCISE OXFORD DICTIONARY, New Edition (revised 1929), also attributes a meaning under c. as *singing, in which all present join.*

suffering, both experience ambivalence toward or even negative expectations of these resources.

In reaction to these feelings, families may fail to involve themselves with treatment planning and planners for their part may turn to overall planning for a sick community instead of a sick child. However, child psychiatrists (even those who are activists in their pursuit of differential planning for the community) seldom engage in successful treatment of the body politic and are even less likely to be found in the corridors of power. The development of the resources necessary to practical planning for children has traditionally been allowed to proceed without interference or stimulus. Some overall planning of community resources is currently being done on a regional basis, but the best of planning still goes to the individual child rather than to the community.

This use of the word *community* has become almost synonymous with references to urban settings, where it is the poverty-stricken black child and his family who are most frequently at the mercy of the academic standoff, bureaucratic battering, and the interminable process-recording of certain family agencies.

The exhaustion of resources takes time, while the passage of time between diagnosis and treatment complicates the planning process still further. The family constellation is altered, the psychic climate changes, and the child grows up. The plan for the use of various resources changes accordingly and only the resources remain fixed—too few in number, too bureaucratic in nature, too academic in attitude, and too close to the dictionary definition of resource as meaning only the possibility of aid, or an *expedient* device.

The planner can be further hampered by self-doubt as to the nature of the dichotomy between the treatment of the internal or psychic economy of the child and the external or social economy. Burgeoning interest in the psychiatric problems of the poor and disadvantaged has led to planning which emphasizes the need to change attitudes toward race, the facts of poverty, and the limiting effects of limited education. However, the planner will find resistance to change in attitudes in a community equal to that in most families. His most effective approach to the use of community resources will be to encourage recognition of the specific dynamics of the problems of a child and his family while moving toward equable solution of the problems of prejudice, housing, education, and an economic place in the sun for a specific family where this is necessary. Overlooking resources which allow development in both areas indicates a serious astigmatism in viewing the problems for which the planning has been instituted.

Evaluation of the child and his family is part of the total evaluative process; evaluation of the provisions the community can make for the needs of this family and this child is an integral part of differential planning. The special knowledge of individual staff members—child psychiatrist, social worker, psychiatric nurse, psychologist, teacher and paraprofessional—defines the practical aspects of what is available. Final decisions are made with an awareness of various checks and balances. The cost of failure to know is high, and the number of variables interfering with effective treatment planning rises precipitously when resources are taken at their face value. Careful planners who would not move precipitously in the course of evaluating the child may fail to take advantage of their membership in their communities. When they could learn about the actual resources available, they do not, and after a splendid start there is a dying fall to differential treatment planning.

Often the planner has not had the training necessary to help him in his evaluation of his community, and early negative experience with the reception of referrals has led to an atrophy of disuse. As the planner increases his own understanding of the continuum of the therapeutic process in relation to resources, he assumes an educational function for those in the community offering services. The providers often lack the perspective to realize how much they may be offering. The planner should take the responsibility for a sophisticated kind of matching of services from the community to the needs of the child, based on such familiar criteria as age, developmental stage, sex, family constellation, and the family's relation to the community. This matching goes beyond stereotypes and is an integral part of differential treatment planning.

Thus, staff of a child guidance clinic may need to have pointed out to them the services available for the retarded, while a school social worker may underestimate the therapeutic role the school is playing in a child's life. Similarly, a child psychiatrist willing to struggle to maintain a borderline adjustment for a child in a less than borderline family may need to explain the classical nature of his treatment plan to the family and to consultants appealed to by the family. In all these cases a person or a setting has a resource, or is using a resource in a way which needs definition for all in order to make it effective.

As differential treatment planning with community resources is carried on, recognition must be given to the therapeutic uses of a given situation at a given time.

Imaginative planning means use of the resources of a community as they actually are, at the same time that daily efforts are made to make each resource yield more than it seemingly can. The ability to make use of the resource as it is and as it might be involves an equally sophisticated view of the child as he is with his problem and as he might be, with disappearing mirrors reflecting the same attributes of family and community.

UNCOVERING THE FACILITATING ENVIRONMENT

"There is no place for philosophers among kings." "Yes there is," I answered "but not for that academic philosophy which fits everything neatly into place. There is, however, another more sophisticated philosophy which accommodates itself to

*the scene at hand and acts its part with polish and finesse. It
is this philosophy that you should use. . . . Give your best
to whatever play is on stage and do not ruin it merely because
something better leaps to mind."*

Thomas Moore, Utopia: Book I

A child grows and his world grows with him. The child's
world may be a facilitating environment or one which blocks
him in his growth; this has long been the concern of people
oriented to the needs of children. Recent work has recognized
the possibility of therapeutically influencing a child's particular
ecological framework. It is our impression that a child-oriented
person can do much to catalyze, create or uncover a facilitating
environment for a child on a communitywide scale. We use
the term *uncovering* to imply the need and process of "digging
out" an asset of the community which is already present but
lies dormant and largely hidden from view. We refer to all
those persons with good understanding of their fellows, with
common sense and honest humanitarianism, who can and do
touch the destinies of individuals among them.

We have chosen to recount here the actual experiences of a
young child psychiatrist as he attempted to dig out the assets of
his community. The setting is a city of about 70,000 people
in a northern state of the Midwest. It is small enough that
there is considerable and inevitable personal contact among
mental health professionals. It lacks some of the problems of
the large urban areas (high delinquency and crime rates,
marked racial and poverty problems) but has a tradition of
provincialism and isolationism. Here, then, is the personal
account of young Dr. X,*** energetic, idealistic, just out of
training—something of a modern-day pioneer.

At the time I elected to go to Central City, I was the only
child psychiatrist in private practice in the state and was

*** Dr. X was a Ginsburg Fellow with the Committee on Child Psychiatry.

working in a catchment area of over 200,000 people. In that first year, much of my time and energy was spent in getting to know many of the people in the helping agencies and the services they provided children. Some of these resource people were homemakers, visiting nurses, Mental Health Center staff, school counselors, physicians, staff at a residential treatment center for retarded children, welfare workers, Catholic Charities staff, juvenile authorities, the University Hospital resources about a hundred miles away, and the nearest state mental hospital.

What proved to be important to learn was not so much the roles these people filled, but the helping people themselves as persons. I got to know that one of them loved working with younger children but tensed up with adolescents, that another was a good organizer and could be counted upon to arrange a comprehensive treatment team, and that a third just needed some reassurance in order to do a splendid job. I learned which person felt bored and was looking for a new approach to the daily problems he faced, which one was mostly bureaucratic and unwilling to risk doing anything different from the conventional pattern established thirty years ago, which one was simply looking for a place to "dump kids."

As I was getting to know these people, so I was getting to be known. I experienced a mutual good feeling among persons in direct contact with children. I decided the best way for me to know them and become known by them was to invite other child-concerned persons into my actual work activities. I saw to it that a child who was having trouble in foster homes was interviewed with his caseworker present; she was allowed to observe several play therapy sessions. A mental health worker became co-therapist in a group of preadolescents; a detective became a member of an ongoing therapy group for hospitalized adolescents. A teacher became a full-time staff member of the hospital's adolescent treatment team. About a dozen people—some from agencies and several private citizens—formed a team to rehabilitate a brain-damaged child and his family. There were many people, interested, concerned people possessing interpersonal skills, who were willing to work, to grow, and to learn with us.

Gradually, things began to sort out and more and more of our efforts began to be channeled in certain directions. Upon reviewing the many visible patients, the amount of anxiety they generated in the community, and the limitations of existing community response, certain high-priority categories of children began to emerge.

Adolescents, of course, headed the list, with problems ranging from drug abuse to schizophrenia, followed at some distance by elementary school children with minimal brain dysfunction and young children with psychoneurotic disorders and behavior problems. Of first importance, it appeared that this community had virtually no facilities for adolescent care. Second, the child with minimal brain dysfunction was just beginning to be diagnosed, let alone to have any program developed for him. Such categories as the retarded child were already covered well by a residential care center, special schooling, a sheltered workshop, and ample diagnostic facilities; the unwed mother's needs were being met; special education programs were functioning in the schools; and the concept of working with entire families was operative in several of the agencies.

Another area of community need that I came to appreciate more and more was that there were all sorts of people, with many kinds of training, occupying a variety of official and nonofficial positions, who were engaged in the business of "counseling," "working with," "placing," "talking to," and in one way or another, attempting to influence children and their families. As I came to know some of these people better, they expressed their needs for supervision and continuing training.

I began a process of feeling my way along, listening to persons working with children and responding to my own sense of engagement with certain issues. Presently there emerged for me these three large areas of community need along with a sense of meeting them. This lay not in "mobilizing community resources," or "grantsmanship," or "selling" the power structure a program. There was much that could be done with the resources and people already at hand.

The psychiatric hospital was willing to provide the staff, training and consultants to start an inpatient adolescent treatment program. Adolescent team members began to take on more responsibility for meeting with families and helping them to communicate and engage with the hospitalized adolescent. We found that therapists working in teams of two or three could deal creatively and positively with most of the families of our disturbed youngsters. It seemed more important for the co-therapists to be comfortable with each other and to communicate well than to have had equivalent training. We were "uncovering" family therapists in nurses, aides, ministers. As staff felt free to learn and develop along lines that were meaningful to them, they brought to bear many spontaneous, creative talents in their performance at the adolescent unit. Psychodrama techniques were especially helpful in developing this potential and as a tool for enhancing meaningful interpersonal interactions.

A "youth-sensitive" chair in the group therapy sessions at the hospital was established. Capable people from the community were invited to come and work with us for up to three months so as to increase their understanding of adolescents, to grow personally, and to become involved with the hospital program. A college counselor, a detective, a priest, a student, a high school counselor have occupied this chair. Each has taken back with him to his own "youth-sensitive" position a clearer understanding of himself and the young people he is dealing with.

Money became available and a halfway house was established for adolescent girls. The Mental Health Center started several adolescent outpatient groups. Drug abuse, a "hot" issue in the community, was attacked by a comprehensive coordinated city effort ranging from clinical treatment to educational approaches to remedying some of the social conditions aggravating the problem. This attack was spearheaded by one of the persons who had occupied the "youth-sensitive" chair.

The children with minimal brain dysfunction had many unmet educational needs. There was no organization to help parents understand the particular needs of these children (emotionally and medically as well as educationally) or to work effectively to bring pressure to bear in establishing the required educational programs. Parents were encouraged to set up a local chapter of the National Association for Children with Learning Disabilities. This group has since made a strong positive impact on the community. They have sponsored programs to educate citizens and have lobbied for special school programs for their children. They have helped each other through sharing the problems that arose out of their children's behavior and the solutions. This was the result of uncovering latent, powerful resources dormant in the community and of then catalyzing a more facilitating environment for children with this handicap.

To respond to the needs and enhance the effectiveness of persons already deeply committed to working with children, a weekly evening workshop was established to which they were all invited. Discussion was stimulated, utilizing mostly role-playing techniques, some videotapes, case presentations, and actual family demonstrations. The workshop has continued to meet with an enthusiastic response.

The above account might have been entitled "Cultivating One's Professional Garden." It suggests that the facilitating environment is not created by organizing a directory of institutions and organizations, or by providing a list of agency phone numbers. Its theme is, *Facilitate around people*.

A WORKING KNOWLEDGE OF COMMUNITY RESOURCES: THREE ILLUSTRATIONS OF TREATMENT PLANNING

Case 1: Battered child in a ghetto community

An abused 18-month-old girl was referred for routine (child) psychiatric consultation. She had been admitted to the hospital with contusions and lacerations of the face after being hit by her 17-year-old mother with a flyswatter. The case was reported to the *Protective Unit of The City Department of Social Services* as prescribed by law, but the recommendation was made that the chief responsibility for work with the mother remain with the *Adult Psychiatry Clinic* to which she was referred at her own request. In addition, it was recommended that the child be followed at the *Child Psychiatry Clinic* on a two-month basis so that the ongoing mother-child relationship could be monitored and appropriate referral made to a *nursery program* in the area within the next year.

The responsibility for the follow-up on the mother's referral for psychiatric help was taken by the Child Psychiatry Clinic, since the Protective Unit had been found to be naive as well as overworked. Follow-up for the child in the Child Psychiatry Clinic was thought necessary as the mother's emphasis in her treatment with the adult psychiatrist was on her own early object loss. Eventual therapeutic intervention was planned in the form of the institution of a day care program. The referral to the *Day Care Center* was made carefully, with emphasis on the Center's experience and resources. The promise of backup services by its Adult Psychiatry and Child Psychiatry Clinics was made to alleviate the anxiety staff felt over the child abuse. Too much emphasis on the psychiatric aspects of the case would have led to rejection of the child as being too seriously disturbed to take into a group of normal children. A benign *employment agency* was persuaded to find the young mother a job that provided her with peer interaction and interest. The Adult and Child Departments collaborated well in the total care of mother and daughter, with interdepartmental conferences regularly maintained throughout the planning and treatment periods.

Case 2: Hyperactive child at a city clinic

A 9-year-old boy was referred with a history of disruptive behavior in the classroom. The findings were highly suggestive of brain injury, but the final differential diagnosis between brain injury and hyperactivity secondary to anxiety and aggressive drives could not be made. The special classes of the *Board of Education* were not available as the IQ fell in the borderline range on psychological testing. In view of the mother's anger at the child's propensity for getting into trouble, she was offered weekly appointments with a social worker at the *Child Psychiatry Clinic.* An attempt was made prematurely to involve the child in a special after-school program, but his attendance was irregular due to his mother's fear that he might enjoy himself. It was noted that the boy strengthened his position with his mother by encouraging her anger at the program by frequent descriptions of games played, trips made, and other activities.

Finally, all clinic visits including those to the after-school program stopped. It was decided follow-up could be best done with the cooperation of the *visiting nurse service,* which scheduled a home visit. The visiting nurse was somewhat taken aback by the mother's negative feelings about the clinic but rallied with interest in the mother's problems. Another home visit was made, and the mother seemed to make good use of the sessions with the visiting nurse. The clinic's inability to offer the mother enough help was explained to the visiting nurse, who finally lost her guilt at doing "better" than the clinic. Subsequent to a final outburst of aggressive feeling, the child was suspended from school. The visiting nurse followed the mother through this period and noted her defense of her son and the displacement of her anger onto the Board of Education. At the nurse's request, the mother and child returned to the clinic, which helped in returning the boy to school. The mother was aware of the clinic's reaction to the Board of Education and the last visit saw the mother interpreting the Board of Education to the clinic. The child settled down at the normal school and continued to show improvement.

This case offers an example of ongoing treatment planning

that was not too rigidly geared to the Clinic's preconceptions. Instead, it was flexibly organized to exploit community resources whenever needed. The acceptance of and working with negative feelings were crucial to the case.

Case 3: Eloping adolescent

A 14-year-old girl was brought to the clinic as an emergency by her mother after having run away from home for the third time. Since it was clear that the family could not offer necessary controls, it was suggested that the mother take her daughter to *Court* as a person in need of supervision so that the mother's real wish to protect her daughter be recognized concurrently with the daughter's wish to be taken care of. In view of the girl's complaints about her mother's poor management of the family budget, the family was referred to a *family agency* by the court. It was judged that the girl could not use direct help, but recommendations were made to *school, court and agency*. The agency pushed hard for individual treatment for the girl; the clinic team felt the agency underestimated the importance of its own role and the positive attitude of the court and overestimated what individual treatment would have to offer.

Agencies can misunderstand one another; they may overestimate or underestimate one another and they may differ radically in their assessment of a case. Such confrontations are especially apt to arise when the collaborating agencies work at different levels. In this case, one agency based its decisions predominantly on factors within the patient, the other concerned itself with the harsh realities of an external existence. Nevertheless, good clinics and good agencies are generally able to run the gamut of understanding successfully.

The case not only served the useful purpose of initiating an ongoing discussion between agency and clinic conducive to improved management of the family situation as a whole, but also established an open channel of communication that augured well for other shared problems in the future.

7

COMMUNICATING THE FINDINGS
AND RECOMMENDATIONS

The mental and moral peculiarities of childhood engage far less than they deserve the attention of most practitioners of medicine, and hence it comes that the treatment of the disorders of early life is to so large a degree a matter of unintelligible routine.

Charles West (1871)

The most skillfully executed diagnostic study and the most thoughtfully formulated diagnostic plan are of little value if they cannot be communicated: first to the family and then to those who will bear the responsibility for putting the therapeutic thought into action.

The process of communication might better be called the art of imparting. Successful delivery of recommendations involves an adequate transmission of the sense of a joint meeting, with all its complicated thinking and painful feeling. Traps for the unwary involve both sender and receiver. The planner is responsible for both, in large part for self and for the nature of the message sent, in smaller part for others and the character of the reception. After the giving and receiving with the accompanying agreement or disagreement comes the third part of the process. This consists either of the joint definition of goals, or a rejection of premise and purpose.

These three steps have to be taken, first by planner and

family, and then by planner and community. In both cases clarity and empathy must precede if clarity and trust are to follow. Resistance to the reception of the message can arise from lack of clarity or empathy in the sending, or as we more often expect, it can arise as the receivers defend themselves against a message whose import they fear.

TO THE FAMILY

The planner must believe that the treatment plan belongs to the family and that an effort is being made to give it over to them. However, there is no realistic plan until reception has been acknowledged. The planner can only advise—the family can consent, demur or confiscate. The planner's message may be received as sent or it may be lost, stolen, strayed or received with distortion.

> A child psychiatrist was consulted by the parents of a boy with learning disabilities, behavior disorder, and hypertrophied tonsils. The mother asked whether having his tonsils out wouldn't alleviate the problems. The boy and parents were seen conjointly, observations were compared, dynamics discussed, and recommendations formulated. The results were carefully explained to the parents, who listened attentively and agreed politely. As they were leaving the mother said, "Now doctor, about the tonsils. Do you think that having his tonsils out . . .?"

Success in communication may depend on positive as well as negative transference: The fear of punishment from her own father may bring the reluctant mother into line, the glimpse of the interpreter as a sympathetic mother may help the unwilling father hear.

The importance of preformed stereotypes among those communicating may relate to different dynamics operating at different levels of consciousness. The WASP family may be ready for the recommendations of the Jewish analyst, or they may not. The black mother may hear the black planner, or she may not. Positive identification with one's "own kind" depends on some attitudes of which one is conscious ("Blacks understand blacks"), and on others which one wishes to keep unconscious ("Blacks may not be as good as whites"). The language may be the same for both parties but nonetheless incomprehensible. Success comes most easily when, from the beginning, planner and family share a common purpose. This may be simply the wish to relieve a child in pain. The agreement to help and be helped comes most readily to those with a previously established ability to trust.

All the techniques to improve communication with families strive for these same goals:

>   ——prevention of misunderstanding
>   —recognition of the nature of neurotic resistance and its handling
>   —establishment of oneness of purpose

Parents will employ their own measures to test the developing relationship. They may ask the planner personal questions. The nature of these queries will make it clear whether they are taking small steps toward establishing a common ground or are moving toward destroying their own trust in the plan. The use of a particular mystique by some planners is a matter of personal style. It must be remembered that adults as patients respond differently from adults as parents. In the latter role, they must react to what they see as the threat of separation from their child. They will not leave him easily, or commit themselves lightly to an unknown situation. They must have some ground for trust, and may actually distrust the charismatic individual.

If more than one person has been involved in planning, a

choice must be made as to whether it is better for one or several planners to meet with the family. If one planner is to represent a team, then the discipline of that person is far less important than the already established relationships which exist, the success of communication achieved, the capacity of the planner to be comfortable with the subtleties of parental relationship, and his ability to focus on the child.

Another necessary decision concerns the way in which the family unit should be broken down and how built up in the course of an interview: parents together, one by one, child alone, or all three together. This will depend in part on the sensitivity of the family's progressive reaction to the process of evaluation, and how it has been observed. In addition, time and timing are important. The length of the session is determined less by the complexity of the situation than by the personalities of those involved. Hopefully, the planner takes this into consideration and shortens or lengthens the planning session accordingly, adding a follow-up visit where necessary. Long sessions assume the characteristics of a marathon which sometimes (but not always) offers families the opportunity to do the necessary work on the spot.

> Mr. and Mrs. C were anxious to have help for their 7-year-old son who was reacting to their demands for success with bedwetting and sleepwalking. They asked few questions and made few remarks. When treatment was mentioned they merely asked "When should he start?" as the mother began putting on his overshoes. It was necessary to continue the interview.

After a long and expensive invasion of privacy, families deserve the presentation of a dynamic formulation, a diagnosis, and a treatment plan. This is hardly covered by asking families if they have any questions. Concrete information is appreciated; conclusions must be supported by data. An anecdote about the observed interaction between parents and child may be illustrative, but may also be downright embarrassing. The friendly anecdote, honestly told, is often hard to come by.

Reference to the history given may be useful, but parroting what parents already know is not. Illustrations which quote parents back to themselves may be necessary to point up contradictions, ambivalence, or the use of denial. The ability to inflict pain without losing the family lies in the ability to respect, to empathize, to lend support along with the confrontation. Planners are usually niggardly about what they tell; if they become overly expansive and obtain pleasure from their own exposition, they may suddenly have the awkward feeling that they are talking to themselves, not to the parents. The avoidance of jargon is essential. The right words have to be found and a common language must be established.

The choice of language is a matter of individual style and common sense. It does not vary too much with the receiver. It is often assumed that persons we see as intelligent and sophisticated naturally share our language, or that the disadvantaged need more "telling." This is nonsense. Ignorance about dynamics, resistance to lack of clarity, and inability to trust are no respecters of class. The problem lies with the planner who feels at home with the rich and, indeed, disadvantaged with the poor. How to make minds meet—this is the problem of the planner.

Where to start, what to tell, and what to leave unsaid involves great sensitivity as well as intuitive, if painfully learned, flexibility on the part of the interpreter. It is best to give the family the benefit of the doubt and start with the assumption that they are listening and can hear. One can shift gears later if necessary. It helps to start with positives; it is reassuring to say that a child is not retarded, not brain injured, or not psychotic. On the other hand, parents may not accept or even hear the reassurance. Indeed, it can happen that they only hear the word *retarded,* or *brain injured,* or *psychotic,* and later in the interview, the realities about their child have to be disentangled from their fantasies. Sometimes parents come to the interpretive interview with an established point of view. They are already convinced of a certain diagnosis and have worked out an appropriate plan. In these situations, cheerful reassurances about the health of the child are not welcome. As we saw in the case of the little boy with the tonsils, certain families cling to a theory of physical illness against all opinion to the contrary. The planner may make his statement and the family hears it, but the preconceived idea which has its roots in individual and family dynamics is not altered.

Where the chief obstacles seem to be guilt and the expectation of blame, the planner attempts to help the family help themselves. They are encouraged to accept feelings about being part of the problem without experiencing immobilizing guilt or feeling a need for defensive denial. Often enough the mother accepts the blame while the father sits back and encourages her to be the victim. If they are to share the therapeutic effort, they must be helped to share the responsibility for what has gone wrong. It is usually extremely important to have the father involved. Unless he is involved—and often painfully so, with some activation of past and present conflicts—he remains an observer.

> A father agreed with the clinician that he was not spending enough time with his son. The following Saturday, he took him to a football game—along with two of his men friends.

While focusing on information for communication, problems inevitably emerge about confidentiality. The course of history-taking may be strewn with statements such as "Of course he doesn't know," and "I have never told him." The child's quick glance at the door or direct question, "Will you tell?" poses the same problem. Facts and feelings which need to be discussed can and should be so labeled in the course of the evaluation. Alternatives of emphasis and focus can then be noted. Families will often respond to the suggestion that "things will not be told" but attitudes and feelings will have to be referred to. Although sometimes the professional's rationalization, "You really want them to know," is just that; at other times parents and child will admit they told something, to have it told. There are things the child does not wish the family told; there are things the planner is not permitted to tell the child. The way around this sometimes involves statements, rather than questions: "I am going to tell your parents *this,* so that they will understand *that.*"

> Mark said little about his family. "My father would hit me if he knew I had told you anything."

Once its dangers are appreciated, however, the problem of handling of confidentiality is as nothing compared to the hazards of giving interpretations, oedipal or otherwise. The more highly sexualized the material to be discussed, the more difficult it is to avoid the glaring implications which interpret themselves. "He is my little man—he takes his father's place." "I feel as if I were starting all over again with her mother." These statements are actually quite provocative. It is sometimes wiser to let them speak for themselves and to discuss their manifest content in a more general context. Where the pathology is less extreme, the normal developmental process for child and family may allow the interviewer to suggest changes in behavior—from a cowardly "he may be a little big to get into bed" to a strong "overcloseness to their father may actually frighten girls at this age."

Where two parents are far apart in their readiness to hear, the focus must be on the "backward" parent. The technique of using diminutives ("It sounds a little confusing," "That may be a little too much") is sometimes justified, sometimes insulting. Perceptive parents and children hear, but they may need to be allowed to save face. More defensive families will use this approach, or have already used it, to minimize distress and symptoms and to indulge with the planner in a dangerous kind of micropsia.

The same care in communication applies to other areas of interaction. Honesty should not be confused with bluntness. Better to say, "You're trying too hard to be a good mother," than "Get off his back." Let the mother say, "You mean I should get off his back?" and she will be pleased with her ability to catch on, better motivated to continue to think and hear. It is always better to lead parents toward finding their own solutions. Their recognition of the planner's ability to move out of the way is a sign of their readiness to come to an agreement with the planner about what to do. This may be particularly important where the therapeutic plan does not involve a recommendation for psychotherapy.

The use of the right word at the right time is important, but a self-conscious use of slang to represent the message is seldom very helpful. Families may use their own vocabulary, and words may be used and reused in mental quotes because of the values they represent, but it is not necessary to "swing."

The less there is to say, the more important it is not to say too much. This is an axiom, and as useful as most axioms. The more confused the facts, the less clear the alternatives, the simpler the presentation must be. However obvious this may be, it is difficult for the most experienced of planners to remain silent while a family cries for absolutes and an end to the balance between "on the one hand—and on the other." The more serious the pathology, the simpler the central facts should be made. The seriousness of the pathology can be stated at once and then dealt with descriptively, or the implications of an initial statement can be developed gradually over several sessions.

The final stage of communication is that part compounded of the planner's skill and art in transmitting and the family's capacity to hear and to learn. It is by far the most difficult stage. Their receptivity is their selective ability, individually and together, to consider the recommendations as they are made. Their consideration represents a first step in their acceptance of a plan for action. The degree of their unwillingness to accept certain aspects of the dynamic formulation measures their resistance to the price they will have to pay for agreement. It also indicates the energy with which they are defending against the reactivation of anxiety and the loss of self-esteem. The solutions to certain problems evoke less guilt than others and these can be discussed first. One moves from the less guilt-provoking problems (those which the parents can most easily accept) to the more difficult ones. The careful listener can often let the parents decide the order in which to consider various aspects of the problems. His grasp of their rating system increases his understanding of them by an appreciable margin.

Whether communication of the plan ends with the transfer of responsibility from planner to family depends on the parents' strength and their ability to move from illness to health with their child. There is a developmental step to be taken from evaluation to treatment. Most parents take this step; in a few cases their refusal to do so and their insistence on their own autonomy dictates a new treatment plan. With the acceptance of the treatment plan by the parents, the coordinator assumes his responsibility for continuity of treatment. Up to that point, the planner must share with the parents the responsibility for follow-through. He must expect and welcome the parents' protests against the plan, so that it can be discussed and defended. Without follow-through on the part of the planner, he may never know why the recommendations were not followed. The result may be tragic for the child and family and so much wasted effort for the planners.

TO THE REFERRING SOURCE AND THERAPEUTIC NETWORK (A REVERBERATING SYSTEM)

It is as difficult to communicate a treatment plan to the community as to a family. The relationships between one setting and another are bound to be complex, particularly where one of them is expected to carry out treatment and take responsibility for the planning. The nature of the relationship in turn affects communication. As is true in laying the groundwork for eventual success in communicating, a specific treatment plan starts at the time of referral. By that time, unsuccessful attempts on the part of the referring agency to do it alone, to find other services, or to avoid any referral may have left their mark. Sometimes careful work with a problem will have brought a family and the referring source to the point where they need and want new services. The success with which an ongoing treatment plan can later be communicated to another agency lies in this beginning, especially where ongoing help from the agency is part of the plan.

As in communication with a family, successful communication with helpers outside the family calls for clarity, empathy, and some agreement as to current and future roles. Agreement on an eventual plan becomes very difficult if the beginning carries with it too much frustration, guilt, negative anticipation, or too many positive anticipations (should these involve denial of the realities of the services available).

> The chief of a Mental Retardation Center called an outpatient clinic to request the admission of a retarded adolescent to a psychiatric ward. On-the-spot planning was hampered by the caller's repeated reference to the existence of a nonexistent inpatient service. His positive anticipation of this service left the referring source angry and frustrated when he had to accept the fact that the service was unavailable.

The end point in planning is the acceptance of a plan; it is very much a part of the referral in private practice, clinic, hospital or agency. The referring source is apt to be saying a number of things in making a referral; if the nonverbal communications are not dealt with verbally, they may endanger the eventual plan.

The first and most obvious implication is: "You do it," which has to be countered by: "We need to know what you have done and what you think—you may well have an ongoing role to play." The setting or agency which is asked to do the planning (including treatment) needs to identify for itself clearly the contributions which must be made and which only it can make. It needs to be equally clear about its own limitations. The staff of this agency will then be able to understand better the kind of self-inventory they are requesting of other services.

The second implication in referring to a treatment setting is: *"You will treat the child,"* which has to be answered by: "Evaluation is not treatment—treatment does not always represent the best approach. Individual and family therapy are not 'higher ordered'—treatment may be contraindicated. You (the agency) have in fact been offering the best therapeutic program for this child—and (most important but least welcome) we will have a look, but you should probably continue." Sometimes the treatment plan is included in the referral: "We cannot see this child as we feel he needs medication. Mrs. M is now anxious for help (usually a gross overstatement) and should be seen on a once-a-week basis."

With so much of the final expectation expressed at the beginning, it is obvious that careful thought and planning, proper conferences, sagacious letters, and wise telephone calls should precede treatment planning at the time of referral. It is unfortunate when too much emphasis is placed on the child and the family and too little time is spent with the referring source or with whatever agencies will have important roles to play in the treatment plan. Communication with these services (school, play groups, court, welfare) is usually maintained through successful consultation, or is painfully established as they evolve appropriate roles through experience with specific cases.

Thus a gap tends to exist between the expectations of the planners (the referring source) and those of the referral whose services they will need. To some extent this gap can be closed by prompt response to the initial request (whatever the eventual time lag for the actual delivery of service), by the courtesy of this response, and by some indication of what will be done immediately. The pressing quality of the needs of those making the referral may well interfere with planning. However, these needs can usually be met, and reality served as well, by written acknowledgment of the referral along with a request for further information. Such information is necessary after a beginning has been made but before a final plan is arrived at. The groundwork for collaborative planning and for carrying out collaborative treatment may be laid during the diagnostic assessment. This requires that the planners keep in touch with the referring source. Collaborative effort will be attenuated when it is assumed that the patient has already been taken care of and the referring source is no longer "wanted." The diminution of self-esteem which follows lack of attention underlies the appearance of the common clinical symptoms of agency irritability, depression, apathy and obstinate withdrawal.

Those who refer children but have no role in the ultimate plan can eventually be reassured if they receive a report which acknowledges their role in the recognition of a problem, outlines the findings, and indicates the (final) solutions. Needless to say, preparation of such a report implies that permission has been obtained from the family.

As an actual plan emerges from the evaluation of the child, it should be discussed with the child and family first, and then brought to the community. It may be necessary to let the family know that part of the plan depends on the availability of resources elsewhere. Nonetheless, if they are to be given their due place in the therapeutic endeavor with the child, preliminary discussion of the basic plan with the family is essential. They must hear it first.

Guided by findings in the diagnostic assessment, the planners should determine who are the essential people to be invited to the initial comprehensive planning conference. This will involve consideration of the agencies to be invited, and levels of staff to be included. Agencies not currently active with a patient or his family may be invited if a significant shift in responsibility for service is anticipated. In such a case, someone at the supervisory level is perhaps the kind of representative who can contribute most to the discussion and the planning. The new agency should be given some preliminary account of the reasons for its participation in the conference. Adjunctive agencies and services may not need to be involved or represented at this point in planning—for example, a tutorial service that is a part of the school or a homemaker service which is part of the social agency.

Appropriate planning must involve the right people. A planning conference must be large enough to include all active contributors, but small enough that each may indeed be heard. It must allow time enough for the exchange of ideas and for plans to evolve. It must become, for this moment in time, a consortium which can assign and accept responsibility for the treatment plan. Thus, it must undertake to establish priorities, designate the coordinator for implementation of the plan, clarify mechanisms for getting the job on its way, and set up feedback channels for successes, difficulties and failures within the plan. This type of treatment planning conference should have covered possibilities for immediate implementation so solidly that its impetus will carry the plan a long way. The need for frequent replanning conferences (which are time-consuming) may indicate faulty coverage at the initial conference.

Where the presumption that the plan will carry a long way

cannot be made, where planning and replanning reflect shifts in living conditions and family and community interrelationships, the unit of time is shortened and the reason for large conferences diminished. Now the coordinator responsible for the continuity of care for a child takes responsibility for working with those immediately necessary to the family and for bringing the others up to date at intervals. Realistically this may end with a breakdown in communication reestablished only at point of crisis. Where possible, the final plans or series of plans should also be brought to the attention of the referring source. Telephone calls and even letters should be substituted for conferences, particularly where there are frequent changes in direction of the plan.

> Hiram, 10 years old, had been followed for a period of time in a clinic in accordance with a treatment plan. Little progress was noted. He was acknowledged to be a sick boy. Telephone conversations with the school established this as a view shared by school and clinic. The only family member who could be seen was the stepmother, who had raised Hiram since infancy. She remained basically unaccepting, although she offered lip service to a revised plan for residential treatment. No steps were taken. In the face of an increase in the severity of the psychotic process, it became crucial to change the original plan for Hiram.
>
> Mother, doctor (planner), two guidance counselors, Hiram, and an assistant principal met together. His stepmother really wanted a plan that would take Hiram out of the home. It was agreed that Hiram would continue at school for roughly a week while a state hospital referral was made. Hiram was reassured that he was not being suspended, but it was made clear that he had to go to the hospital. One of the two state hospitals under consideration was chosen and the planner was to meet with the stepmother and father (who had only been seen once).
>
> This appointment was changed once at the father's re-

quest and then canceled. The designated state hospital was said not to have the expected program and intake staff were not available by phone during the next week. The mother then requested immediate state hospital placement through the guidance counselor, saying that the father would not come in—all by phone. This request became the final plan outlined in the short summary sent to the state hospital. A copy of this summary was to be sent to the school, as multiple releases had been signed by the stepmother.

The need for continuing communication of the planner's plan and the transmission and transfer of this plan to agencies in the community is as essential as the transmission of the plan to the family. Agreement is the final stage of both communication and treatment planning.

8

TREATMENT PLANNING IN PRACTICE

> *The theory of medicine belongs to memory and intellect, the practice to the imagination. Physicians of great learning are prone to be poor practitioners while those of low intelligence who learnt only a few things in medical school may be successful.*

> Juan de Dias Huarte y Navarro (1570)

In every medical discipline, rational treatment planning involves a definition of specific therapeutic goals. In each case, these goals are based upon the diagnostic evaluation. Once defined, the method or methods of intervention which under the existing circumstances are best suited to accomplish these goals must be selected. In the field of child psychiatry, however, the present state of our knowledge often permits only rough correlations between diagnostic findings and treatment methods. Much depends on what resources are available, and it is not always possible to specify a single "treatment of choice" for a particular child with a given diagnosis.

FIVE TYPES OF THERAPEUTIC INTERVENTION

As an aid to systematic thinking in treatment planning, goals for therapeutic intervention can be divided into five types, according to which aspect of the child's existence is identified as the prime target for change. At any given moment during therapeutic work with a family the treatment plan usually strives to achieve two or more of these goals:

1—Intrapsychic modification
2—Alteration of intrafamilial functioning
3—Alteration of peer-group interaction
4—Modification of the child's school or community adjustment
5—Removal of the child for a period of time to an altogether different environment

It is essential that these goal priorities be made very clear. Clarity aids in complex decision-making later in treatment and can render the chosen therapeutic interventions more efficient. In the face of school refusal, for example, choice of the first-priority goal can lead naturally from diagnostic thinking to rational choice of therapeutic methods. Five hypothetical cases illustrate this point.

In the first case, diagnostic study revealed that the child's unwillingness to attend a school had to do with long-standing and deeply rooted anxieties about separation from his mother. These problems were related to traumata in infancy. The therapeutic goal of intrapsychic change in the child dictated that the optimum intervention would be individual psychotherapy or psychoanalysis.

In a second situation, the diagnostic study uncovered a family imbalance in which the parents used their child to avoid facing marital conflicts. The family shared an unconscious fear that some disaster would result if conflict was brought into the open. What the child perceived consciously as a fear of school was in fact his inability to move freely away from his parents into a school setting without anxiety about the outbreak of violence at home. Here the therapeutic task involved alteration of family functioning to relieve the intrafamilial pressure on the child;

family therapy or couple therapy seemed the most appropriate way to accomplish that goal.

A third case of school refusal occurred in a latency boy who had never known his father. Worse, he lacked a close relationship with any man to support the development of his masculine interests. His fears of school developed after he had become the scapegoat of his classmates. He was teased for avoiding rough sports and for trying to be "teacher's pet." In this situation, peer-group rejection precipitated regression in a vulnerable child. The therapeutic goal here might be to help this boy feel more secure with his peers and to counteract his tendency to take shelter with a protective maternal figure. With such a goal in mind, the clinical team might recommend activity group therapy or a Big Brother, as well as consultation with school personnel.

In the fourth case, diagnostic investigation revealed that the child had a specific reading disability and that his fear of school resulted from a problem with his teacher. His inattentiveness, hyperactivity and poor performance—all symptoms of a mild dyslexia—had led to his becoming identified as the "bad child" in her class, and she had resorted to harsh punishments to deal with him. A first goal of treatment had to be modification of the school environment in a way that would both prevent further trauma and meet the child's needs. This might take the form of intensive work with his teacher or could involve transfer to a more sympathetic and specialized classroom situation. Simultaneously chemotherapy could be initiated.

In the fifth case, an adolescent boy came to professional attention because of his failure to attend school. The truant officer went to the home to investigate. When the mother mentioned casually that her son spent long periods locked up in his room and slept with knives under his pillow, he referred the boy for diagnostic evaluation. The boy was found to have been suffering from a paranoid psychotic reaction for months. The family had coped with the problem by massive denial;

they simply ignored the boy's bizarre habits and gave up all attempts to set appropriate limits. Hospitalization seemed the only acceptable alternative, since this boy responded to his delusions of persecution by threats of violence and the family seemed completely unable to deal with him. After the boy was hospitalized, attempts were made to involve the family in casework.

These five situations have been somewhat oversimplified in order to emphasize the role of choice of priorities in treatment planning. However complex the clinical situation, it remains important to clarify goal priorities on the basis of available diagnostic information.

A carefully designed treatment plan can incorporate a sequence of different goals. For example, the diagnostic team might conclude that in the third case, the boy could not enter a peer group without getting the other boys to attack him. Nor could he accept a positive relationship with a man until he had at least partially worked through his ambivalent feelings and distorted fantasies about men. Therefore, a relatively brief period of intensive individual psychotherapy which could focus on these intrapsychic problems should be recommended to prepare him for referral to a group or a Big Brother.

Treatment planning does not stop with the initial therapeutic interventions. During the course of work with a given child, periodic reexamination of goals and the progress thus far attained can prevent prolongation of a particular form of therapy beyond the point of diminishing returns or, more serious still, beyond the point where the therapy creates more problems than it solves.

For example, in the fifth case, the adolescent had recovered from his acute psychotic symptoms after a few months of treatment. At the same time, with the help of their caseworker, his family members had given up enough of their denial to be ready to participate seriously in future therapy. At this point, the boy was transferred to day care treatment and was permitted to spend nights at home with his family. His individual psycho-therapy continued but now, in an effort to achieve more con-structive communication among the family members, family therapy sessions were also scheduled. Had inpatient care been continued beyond the necessary interval, the adolescent struggle for independence might have been blocked, possibly increasing the risk of secondary gains from being "sick" and reinforcing chronic or recurrent psychotic regression as a permanent life style.

There are times when it may become appropriate to termi-nate or to shift to an alternative mode of therapeutic interven-tion: (1) when the current therapy has achieved its goal; (2) when the child's reality situation changes, rendering the on-going treatment inappropriate or unnecessary; or (3) when the child moves into a new phase of psychic development that requires suspension or modification of the treatment approach. Thus, sequential shifts in treatment goals, with corresponding shifts in therapeutic recommendations, can be as flexibly varied as the evolving needs of the case require, so long as each goal can be clearly defined as the most appropriate at that point in time and then implemented by a suitable mode of intervention.

Rather than attempt to match children who present a com-plex combination of healthy and disturbed personality facets with an equally diverse array of outpatient resources, we have chosen to develop certain guidelines which can be used for sound treatment planning in any setting. The need for imagi-nation, creativity and flexibility, which has been repeatedly stressed in this report, remains an indispensable prerequisite of practical treatment planning. In our view, these qualities equal in importance the professional competence of the person(s) eventually charged with the treatment of the referred child.

OUTPATIENT TREATMENT

One of the first decisions a treatment planner has to make is whether his patient can remain in his home environment or he has to be removed from it in order to be effectively helped. Outpatient treatment can mean referral to a child guidance clinic, to a child psychiatry department in a medical school or hospital, to an appropriate private clinician, to a family agency with trained personnel able to carry out the necessary treatment, to specially trained educators, or to other community resources. Flexibility of planning demands that the therapist must be prepared to use any or all of these resources which might best suit a particular patient and family. Such multiple therapeutic approaches include parent counseling, family therapy, group therapy, behavior modification, drug therapy, environmental manipulation, remedial education, and individual psychotherapy. The planner's choice will depend on the child's needs, the personnel and facilities available, economic, geographic, religious, cultural, parental, and other environmental factors.

Outpatient treatment is appropriate for the child who needs specialized help to support his healthy developmental strivings but does not need to be removed from the scene of an acute or chronic stress situation. This type of treatment is also suitable for patients who require regular supervision of a drug regimen or who are best served by continuous contact with psychiatric, psychological, or special educational services over many years. Especially where intrapsychic roadblocks have caused a partial developmental arrest in the child or have brought about regression with symptom formation, outpatient psychotherapy is the treatment of choice.

The suitability of such outpatient treatment is contingent *first of all* upon a correct assessment of the child's assets and liabilities—in brief, on the diagnosis. The clinician must decide whether the child is able to cope satisfactorily with his environment during treatment. Severely disturbed children who constantly provoke negative reactions from those about them, or whose perception of reality is too distorted, may need a sheltered or specialized setting if they are to benefit from treatment.

Second, the success of outpatient treatment will depend in large measure upon the ability of the child's family, along with his broader environment, to provide him with everyday material and emotional supplies, intellectual stimulation and age-appropriate recreation. Thus such treatment usually involves work with the patient's parents, his school teachers and whoever else is meaningfully involved in his upbringing. The therapist needs to consult with the school and the parents on the practical issues of how to handle the child. Otherwise he becomes a person who has no influence on the youngster's environment.

A third important factor in treatment planning is the availability and quality of mental health services and personnel. If several outpatient resources are available, a variety of considerations such as costs, geographic location and the like may determine where the child and his parents will be referred. The special interests of various professional persons and agencies can also be considered when referring a child.

Finally, the child's own motivation for treatment, as well as his predilections and preferences (in the case of an older child), constitutes *a fourth factor* of major importance in treatment planning. Over and above the child's motivations, the fit between the personality characteristics of the potential treater and those of the child can have a positive or negative effect upon the child's willingness to be helped. This factor needs to be taken into account in treatment planning.

Under optimal circumstances—that is, when the diagnosis for the child implies a good prognosis, when his parents are cooperative, when services and professional personnel are available and the child is motivated for treatment—treatment planning does not require any lengthy soul-searching. It is only a matter of choosing the best among available good alternatives.

When only three out of the four factors are positive, however, the treatment recommendations require more thought. To give a few examples: What to recommend for a well-motivated neurotic latency child whose parents are dead set against psycho-therapy? What about the boy at puberty who asserts his independence by refusing to come for treatment? Where to find help for a needful and willing but financially strapped family if there is no outpatient facility available for low-income families? In such circumstances, treatment recommendations will depend on careful weighing of the positive and negative factors present.

When only two out of the four conditions appear favorable for outpatient management, treatment planning becomes the kind of challenge that may call upon all the ingenuity, flexibility, creativity and imagination of the planning team. For instance, in the third case of school refusal described earlier, (the latency boy lacking a father), assume that the boy is well motivated while his mother shows a paranoid distrust of any "interference" with her child. The planning team learns, however, that his mother has a long-standing relationship with a local minister. This man is aware of the problem but lacks experience and training in work with young children. Impressed by the minister's warmth and concern, the team offers to provide consultation to him. If the mother can be brought to agreement, they will work with him in developing a relationship with the boy. At a conference with a representative of the planning team at the church, the mother receives sufficient support from her minister to accept the plan. Later, at her minister's urging, she is able to allow her son a wider range of activities with his peers.

If the pro-to-con ratio of factors is only one to three, it is likely that treatment in an outpatient facility will not be effective for unusual circumstances. Where outpatient treatment is the only available modality, at times it can be used to help prepare parents and child to accept temporary inpatient treatment, foster home placement, or other more long-term custodial care.

In our second case of school refusal, suppose that the covert marital tensions which had led to the child's symptom were rigidly fixed in the parents, that they resisted any treatment for themselves or the child, and that no local agencies of any kind had had positive dealings with the family. Such a child, isolated from his peers and held almost entirely under the sway of a neurotic family interaction, could not seek help without parent approval. Under these conditions, the planning team might confront the parents with this alternative: Either they make other plans for the child, such as placement in a residential treatment setting, or it is likely that he will be removed from the home by the state authorities for chronic truancy.

The lack of treatment facilities, of diversified educational and treatment settings, of treatment modalities, and of personnel has often led the clinician to refer a child to the only facilities or personnel available. There is a tendency for him to do this even though these services are not suitable or equipped to give the youngster the help he needs. Treatment facilities involved in such referrals have sparked vigorous attempts to redress these shortcomings. As the number and kinds of resources and personnel increase, treatment planning becomes more purposeful, and the achievement of a viable referral more realizable. But the planner-therapist must still be aware of his own bias: The treatment techniques with which he is most familiar are likely to be what he does best and trusts most. There is the danger of fitting the patient to this preferred technique of treatment rather than seeking the treatment of choice for that patient.

DAY CARE TREATMENT

It has been said that therapy is the technical use of human influence. The most important tool in reaching and helping a troubled child, whether individually or through a team approach, is our relationship to him. Through such a relationship, and with the skill and experience of the treatment providers, we hope to stimulate a child's interest, participation, and wish to achieve within his environment. There are times when one person, no matter how skillful, who spends several hours a week with a child cannot provide enough human influence to effect constructive change. This may be true for many reasons. Among them might be (1) a child's often-entrenched and abrasive neurotic interaction with his parents and siblings, and theirs with him; (2) the family's chronic, unrelenting, often highly charged, wearing battle for control (an interruption of these patterns may help both child and parent to review their relationship in a more sober and realistic light); or (3) the child's failure at school, academically or socially. Each situation calls for special education or tutoring tailored to the patient's abilities and needs. Only in this way can he be spared the humiliating experience of chronic failure among his peer group. A child who continues to be deprived of so vital a source of mastery and self-esteem may withdraw emotionally or intellectually, or he may resort to less desirable ways of attracting his teacher's attention and of evoking the awe of his peers.

On the other hand, inpatient treatment may be inadvisable for the child in one of these situations on several grounds: (1) The parents must be kept involved in a child's daily life in order to motivate them (for their own relief of pain if for no other reason) to make necessary modifications in their attitudes and methods of dealing with him. (2) Even under the best circumstances, removal of a child from his parents often gives the child a feeling of rejection and the parents a sense of failure. It arouses strong feelings of anger, disappointment and guilt. (3) In the case under consideration the child functions reasonably well within the family unit and derives considerable security from it, but is a disaster in the school and neighborhood.

With some of these considerations in mind, a therapeutic day care center may be the recommendation of choice in the treatment plan. Through much of his day, such a center will offer the child a controlled environment that can both gratify his needs and protect him against his own impulses and actions. The center will provide four general areas of therapy and interaction with the child and his family: (1) education; (2) occupational and recreational therapy; (3) group or individual therapy; and (4) parent counseling. This setting will allow the child to work in much smaller groups with more intensive individual attention from adults than is possible in a regular school setting. Optimally, the child is given room for experimentation in how to get along with people and the opportunity to test out various ways of reacting. Structure, controls and limits are available so that he derives the security that comes from knowing and understanding the rules. He will learn that these rules, and the adults who administer them, are predictable, consistent and dependable, and that these adults will help him control his feelings and actions at times when he cannot control them himself. For some children, this may represent an entirely new experience.

Day care treatment can help some families master their separation anxiety and the fear that everyone will act out their strong ambivalent feelings. Often, a more total and permanent removal of the child from his home can become bearable only after a preparatory period in the day center. Thus day treatment can serve as a two-way intermediary between a residential setting and home: as a prelude to complete removal from the home and as a means of achieving partial return to the home after a period of placement.

The development of day treatment programs is assuming high priority throughout the nation. Day treatment typifies the principles of community mental health by providing a partial and limited therapeutic atmosphere which does not remove the child from his home. Since these programs utilize the therapeutic principles that were developed in psychiatric hospitals and residential treatment centers, further discussion of treatment planning for their use will be undertaken along with our review of inpatient and residential treatment facilities.

TREATMENT PLANNING FOR THE
CHILD AWAY FROM HOME

The child is best away from home when his caretakers cannot modify their interaction with him sufficiently to effect or allow change. Placement in a therapeutically designed and controlled environment may then become the major recommendation of the treatment planner. For a period of time, a therapeutic milieu is necessary to replace some or all of the child's daily life experiences.

The range of therapeutic placements extends from foster and group homes and day care or day treatment centers through therapeutic boarding schools, residential treatment centers, and inpatient psychiatric hospital facilities, to correctional institutions. At either end of this spectrum—foster homes or correctional institutions—psychiatric treatment is likely to take the form of consultation services only. In the middle range of services, however, it is likely to provide a strong therapeutic force in shaping the program itself.

It is obvious that the choice of facility should be "titrated" to the youngster's needs. For example, the child who is reacting to a pathological family situation may require foster home placement, that is, a parallel family to provide a corrective living experience for him. On the other hand, the youngster may be unable to tolerate close family interactions without provoking, eloping, or acting out his problems in other ways. This child would require a more controlled setting in which family interactions were diluted rather than replicated. In certain instances, correctional institutions oriented toward the severely acting-out delinquent are necessary. Under optimal conditions, these institutions will offer a highly structured environment which emphasizes behavior control and into which therapeutic principles (via psychiatric consultation) may be built for the individual youngster and the group.

Psychiatric treatment away from home is principally represented in the middle range of programs; the day treatment, inpatient and residential treatment facilities for children. The sharp differences in the latter two, which involve treatment away from home, have begun to blur as each has tended to absorb the characteristics of the other, and these, in turn, are shared with the newer day treatment programs.

Because of the diversities which exist among these programs, it is difficult to speak of one model treatment plan. However, certain guidelines for therapeutic planning do exist. While their relative emphasis and application might vary from program to program and from case to case, they are based on needs common to all severely disturbed children. The specific therapeutic strategies designed for each child thus share three broad features: (a) separation from home, (b) therapeutic milieu, and (c) psychotherapy within the milieu.

Day treatment obviously constitutes a partial separation. It seeks to provide a manageable degree of interaction between the child and his outside environment without removing him from it completely. Separation may take place during school hours, after-school hours, or weekends; this is determined on the basis of which part of the child's relationships, with parents and siblings or schoolteachers and classmates, most needs to be interrupted and reworked in a therapeutic setting.

In other situations, separation may be complete rather than partial. For example, in some cases of acute crisis, a temporary separation involving a short stay in the hospital may be the major factor in effecting improvement. It may simply allow time for the child and family to reconstitute and for a definitive treatment plan to be formulated. The plan can then be carried out largely on an outpatient basis or in a foster boarding placement or day treatment center. In most serious cases, however, separation from conflict is not in itself a solution but rather creates the conditions under which actual treatment can become operable. Within the setting recommended it becomes possible to "titrate" the child and *his* community, that is, his family and school, so that pathological interactions can be brought down to manageable levels and subjected to therapeutic influence.

It is important to emphasize that a truly therapeutic milieu is not static. It is more than a set of rules and procedures or a collection of activities, and even more than a "hygienic atmosphere." Essentially it provides a setting within which a variety of therapeutic factors can be integrated as part of the child's life space. The dosage of treatment can then be individualized and tailored to the youngster's current needs, abilities and tolerances. In this way, the institutional staff can shape and control the milieu for the individual child; within this framework the child's contact with adults and peers and his activities can be regulated according to plan. The therapeutic milieu allows for a measured response from the environment when the child reproduces his previous behaviors and tries to elicit certain responses from those around him.

One important aspect of the therapeutic milieu has been referred to as the "corrective emotional experience." It makes available to the child experiences with new people who do not respond to him as did his family members and others he has known in the past. In this way he can learn new patterns of interaction. However, there is a limitation built into this concept involving timing and the child's receptivity to the "corrective emotional experience." While some change can be effected by patterning and structuring his life so that corrective relationships are continuously provided, often this is enough only at a later stage of treatment, when therapy has uncovered and removed his internal need to repeat symptomatic behaviors endlessly. It is at this point that the youngster with ego dysfunction is most apt to profit from corrective emotional experiences.

Individual and/or group psychotherapy is offered in most modern day care, residential, and inpatient centers for children. In some institutions, all children are in therapy throughout their stay. In other settings the children who can best use psychotherapy are selected, while in still others, children may be introduced to formal psychotherapy at that stage of their stay when it is felt they are most ready to utilize it. The form of therapy varies according to the particular needs of the child patient. However, so many of these children are suffering from various ego disturbances that traditional descriptive terms as "uncovering" or "supportive" are really not applicable to the psychotherapy given them. In any case, children in these institutions usually need a sensitively balanced combination of both techniques.

For some children psychotherapy may remain largely confined to the office. It may be given others, for the most part, on the ward during crises when immediate availability of the therapist is important. His first-hand knowledge of an incident may allow the therapist to interpret and explain to the child the relationship of cause and effect, of action and reaction; and to do so on the spot, before the child has had a chance to distort the incident and convince himself that the distortion is true.

THE FACTOR OF INSTITUTIONAL "TRANSFERENCES"

As one example of the unique interlocking function of these two modalities of treatment, psychotherapy and milieu, we may consider the "transference" potential which the institution provides. The child who is separated from his family, and thus from the original partners in conflict, reexperiences and reenacts these conflicts within the institution. As patterns emerge, the child tends to seek transference figures within the institution with whom to reenact the old conflicts. He relives the past with this new cast of characters—the staff of the unit. Often the recorded events of the daily life of a child in day care, residential, or inpatient treatment can be construed as a narrative; such data read carefully, with meticulous attention to detail, reveal the history of the disorder, the major conflictual figures in the illness, and the specific meanings of the child's pathological behavior and defense. The transference behavior of the child toward institutional figures (including the psychotherapist) provides a diagnostic key to the nature and origins of the emotional disorder. It is, in addition, a thera-peutic instrument for effecting change in personality through insight and corrective emotional experience. The therapeutic potential of the milieu should be utilized fully. To do this, the psychotherapist, child care workers, and other specialists who constitute the child's clinical team must collaborate closely through an exchange of daily clinical observations and the development of mutually reinforcing therapeutic methods.

THE INSTITUTIONAL TEAM AT WORK

It is important for the treatment team to evolve tentative goals and approaches just before or at the time of the child's admission to the program. At their first meeting, the team should evaluate the referral and intake material and review the clinical picture and the dynamics of the child. The psy-chotherapist may discuss the diagnosis, outline the psycho-pathology, and formulate dynamics, relating the traumatic events in the child's life and his developmental experience up to the present symptoms. He may also discuss the degree of disturbance of various ego functions, with reference to specific areas of conflict, fixation and regression. From their knowl-edge of the role the child has played in interlocking family defenses, it may be possible for the team to make educated guesses and attempt to predict certain behaviors within the program—for example, with whom and how the child will recreate his old conflicts.

A broad master plan may be tentatively formulated that in-cludes long-range goals—what kind and how much change the team anticipates in the child's symptom picture and his un-derlying personality structure. The team may also consider how long it may take to accomplish these objectives, and whether the child will most likely return to live with the family and go to public school, or go to an intermediate boarding situation, or to a permanent foster or adoptive home. (Some plans may even establish a discharge date at the time of admission.) Various other general considerations may be discussed, such as the amount and form of contact to be maintained between the institutional staff and the child's community—his home and school. The form and type of psychotherapy, the use of drug therapy, and the milieu program for the child may also be tentatively outlined. Above all, the prescription for treatment is a changing one, and this master plan will be reviewed and revised periodically.

Of course the preadmission diagnostic information is of limited usefulness to the therapeutic team in the program. In the usual evaluation the child's specific disturbances are often not comprehensively covered. Moreover, the evaluation rarely indicates how the team should manage these disturbances. The team usually needs to know more about the child than is provided in the history, in order that pathological behaviors may either be prevented or managed most effectively. The team must decide how to group the child with other children, both on the living unit, in school, and in activities. It must determine which management techniques might be useful and which should be avoided, how the child's major symptoms should be handled and what attitudes should be taken toward certain symptoms. This assessment must be based in part on the diagnostic evaluation. Specific kinds of information are needed: interactions of the child with siblings and peers, his attitudes toward them, their reactions to him, forms of discipline and restrictions used by the parents, and the child's differential response to these. Staff of some programs attempt to make the formal diagnostic information come alive for them by making visits to the child's "natural" settings, his

home and public school, where they can observe him interacting.

A number of additional questions may be posed at this
conference: Will the child react to the initial period of separation from the family with relief, anxiety or sadness? Or will
he react with defenses against these affects? Should one help
certain affects emerge? When will he begin to recreate his
symptom pattern?

To answer these questions definitively, the team must actually
study the living child. They thus proceed stepwise from pre-
dictions based on the diagnostic and historical material to
actual observations and experiences with the child.

The first two or four weeks after the child is admitted to
the program are usually a period of assessment. During this
period the child is slowly being introduced into the group
and the program. Gradually the diagnostic phase overlaps
and merges with the first phase of treatment. It is also a
period during which the team gets to know the child and he
gets to know them. It is the moment to start treatment planning. The team begins to observe the levels at which the child
functions. They learn what they can expect from him and
what specific problems he plays out, which practical techniques
work and which do not. Some inpatient and residential institutions employ a special Admissions Unit in which to observe the child during the first few weeks in order to decide
the permanent unit into which he will fit best. Other institutions, especially the smaller ones, prefer not to employ this
approach. They feel that as the child adjusts himself to the
Admissions Unit, a transfer will require another major read-
justment and an additional reassessment later.

In order to make the best use of this initial period in the
program, it is important that a second planning conference
be held two to four weeks after admission. Its purpose is to
review the initial approach and to add a second set of data to
that obtained earlier from the referral source, in order to

shape a more complete therapeutic prescription. Now the staff knows how the child responds in a group of children, how he behaves with older and younger children, how he relates himself to adults in a variety of situations. If testing for specific educational capacities was done in the intramural school, the teacher can now plan a more definite school program. The milieu staff may have specifically identified certain "traps" set by the masochistic, the seductive, or the paranoid child, and can decide when and how to maneuver to avoid these traps—perhaps when to take a sympathetic stand or when to confront the child with his behavior. To some extent, then, techniques of intervention can now be standardized.

With a better understanding of the child's functioning, the team can determine needs and priorities in a more definitive sense than before. That is, they can intervene actively with certain symptoms and behaviors while leaving others alone or selectively using different approaches. Children requiring treatment away from home usually have multiple diffuse problems rather than single encapsulated problems. While avoiding gaps and loopholes in treatment on the one hand, it is important, on the other, not to surround the child with too many treatments at once, particularly in the early stages of residence. The strategic timing of interventions is crucial; it is analogous to the timing of a physician postponing an operation which his patient needs until other medical problems have been brought under control. With the child psychiatric patient, the team may decide to focus on the management of tantrums and panic while leaving his learning problems alone for some weeks. At the dynamic level, they may decide to isolate the child's dependent needs from his aggressive conflicts and to handle each separately. Thus, at first he might be allowed to sit on the lap of his schoolteacher and be read to, while asked to make little effort himself. The same tactic might be inappropriate and contraindicated at a later period in treatment.

Some children communicate best in groups and some in individual situations, some with male staff and some with female. Both the therapist and the milieu staff now attempt to find in what situations this child most readily exhibits and confides his fears, worries and concerns. The initial phases of psychotherapy are discussed and are related more definitively to the milieu management. Finally, the treatment planner brings together the observations, summarizes the data, and defines more specifically focused tactics and goals for team members. Some decisions may involve his own and others' roles in the child's life during his stay in the institution.

The primary goal of day care and residential treatment is always to return the child to normal family and community life. If the treatment plan envisions the eventual return of the child to his own family, the parents should also be involved in order to be effective and maintain good results. It will be necessary to help them modify some of their attitudes, change certain aspects of their behavior, and understand their own feelings better. If this is accomplished, the environment will not be so disturbing to the child and his behavior will be less disruptive to the parents and family. They will need help in exploring their feelings about the child and his illness, in understanding the meaning of the child's symptoms, in learning better how to be consistent, and in working through the guilt feelings they have over the part they may have played in the child's illness. Optimally the family unit will function more smoothly when the child returns to normal family living.

TREATMENT PLANNING IN THE PEDIATRIC HOSPITAL

The child away from home in the pediatric setting may exhibit behavioral or emotional difficulties. This presents related problems of planning. If the child psychiatrist is an active member of the pediatric staff, he may become involved in a comprehensive diagnostic evaluation of the sick child admitted to the inpatient service and participate in the total treatment.

In treatment planning, overriding considerations may determine urgent priorities. For example, even though psychological factors may well appear to play an important role in the genesis of a child's abdominal pain, it may not be possible to rule out surgery for an acute condition. An exploratory laparotomy may then properly be undertaken on the ground that "it is better to be safe than sorry." Situations arise where the psychiatrist may have to defer to the decision of other physicians for a maneuver he may believe unnecessary or even too traumatic an experience for the child.

Open discussion and exchange among those physicians engaged in the joint diagnosis and treatment planning are vital. Their importance cannot be overemphasized. These professionals must be willing to look at all views with dispassionate objectivity free of rancor or competitive strivings. Without this objectivity, the needs of the child may become lost.

With adequate discussion, a comprehensive picture of the child and his total needs will emerge. This will lead to agreement among the responsible physicians. In its wake, three possible ways of involving the child psychiatrist or some member of his clinical team may be considered.

First: Primary clinical responsibility may be delegated to the child psychiatrist. The details of the plan for specific psychiatric and psychotherapeutic care are then worked out by the psychiatric service. If the child remains in the hospital, the pediatrician carries on as consultant. Within this structure, the child psychiatrist carries primary responsibility for working with the nursing, recreational, educational and other hospital personnel who handle the day-to-day care of the patient. By and large, when children are admitted to a pediatric setting for clarification of diagnosis and are assigned to Child Psychiatry for primary clinical responsibility, they do not remain in the hospital for any length of time. At times, however, the psychiatric treatment is started while the child still occupies a pediatric bed. This may be dangerous for the child, since what is acceptable to the current pediatric resident may be resented by the next house officer to rotate on to the ward!

Second: Primary clinical responsibility resides with the pediatric service, while the child psychiatrist continues as consultant and advisor. This can be an exceedingly important element in the child's total therapeutic regimen. It calls for great skill, patience, sensitivity and compassion on the part of the psychiatric consultant. For example, he may be called upon to help a pediatric resident or a student nurse deal with the fears of a child facing death, and to teach the trainee how to support whatever emergency defense the child can marshal at the moment. To do this without conveying the covert insult that one is "treating" the young physician or nurse may well tax the child psychiatrist's consultative and therapeutic skills. In some situations where the primary clinical responsibility remains with the pediatric service, the contribution of the psychiatric consultant is to help the parents handle their fears about the outcome of the child's illness, whether these concerns are based on reality or not.

Third: There are cases in which a decision is made to share basic clinical responsibility between the two services—pediatrics and child psychiatry. Such a decision is most apt to be made where the clinical diagnosis is ulcerative colitis, anorexia nervosa, or severe asthma. Children with severe psychophysiological disorders need the best coordinated team approach that can be devised along with direct psychotherapeutic involvement of the child psychiatrist. To render the best care to the child there must be close collaboration of the several professionals. This implies agreement on decisions and cooperative planning and communication at all stages. This task is always more difficult to accomplish on a ward in a teaching hospital, for there is a built-in rotation of resident pediatricians, attending pediatricians, medical students and student nurses.

When the child is in the hospital for a relatively long time, the assigned therapist and the senior nursing personnel on the ward become the most knowledgeable professional people on the case. Early in the treatment, guidelines must be set up, functions and roles discussed and established and, where possible, final authority designated for decision-making. Each member of the team must strive for free communication, avoid power struggles, and maintain a respect for the validity and dignity of his professional colleagues. The smoother clinical working arrangements which result are of the greatest benefit for both the child patient and his parents.

9

MISCONCEPTIONS ABOUT DIAGNOSIS AND TREATMENT

Long before physicians had conceived the plan of correcting the false ideas and feelings of a lunatic by purgatives, or the cranial depressions of an idiot by bleeding, Spain had produced several generations of monks who treated with the greatest success all kinds of mental diseases without drugs, by moral training alone. Certain regular labors, the performance of simple and assiduous duties, an enlightened and sovereign volition, watching constantly over the patients, such were the only remedies employed. "We cure almost all our lunatics," said the good fathers, "except the nobles, who would think themselves dishonored by working with their hands."

Philippe Pinel—quoted by
Édouard Seguin (1866)

PATIENT AND CLINICIAN

Families and their children coming for professional help usually have certain preconceptions and misconceptions. These tend to be modified in the course of the evaluation. Clinicians have their misconceptions as well. These change over the years in work with family after family as well as during the study of any given child and his family.

The clinician, the setting, and the plan that evolves often trigger the explosion of stereotyped ideas within the patient

146

and the family. Transference reactions may involve the clinician and any or all of the family members seen. When such strong reactions occur without recognizable motivation, the family may well become confused.

Thus the hospital can be seen as sterile, as pain-filled, or as the Great Medical Center in the Sky. The clinic may become a place to wait, the private office a place for the rich, while the agency is confused with welfare, social workers, West Side Story, and the Salvation Army.

The clinician may be regarded as Rasputin or Dr. Kildare, as stern judge or indulgent permissivist, as beaurocrat or lecturer, Solomon or Moses. These stereotypes tell a great deal about what the patient and the family want and fear, but if modification of such misperceptions and the attendant feelings does not take place, no effective treatment plan can be agreed upon.

Once the plan is evolved, a new set of distortions appears. Sometimes short-lived, these reactions are clearly experienced as fantasies. The stress on school planning raises the specter of military school or a school for the retarded, the discussion of therapy at home raises the question of hospitalization, the suggestion that no treatment is necessary is seen as a refusal to help. Fantasies of rescue are as difficult to handle as fantasies of abandonment. This is the point at which verbal and nonverbal skills may most effectively combine for useful communication.

Recognition of the nature of the distortion can sometimes help in the therapeutic push toward completion of planning. Instant insight is unlikely. On the other hand, within the therapeutic milieu of treatment planning, parent and child may now make previously forbidden connections on a number of counts. Such connections couldn't be arrived at without full understanding of transference. Only the very young clinician expects awe, gratitude and constant satisfaction from his patients. Only a few continue to expect their patients to be accurate, articulate and selective, merely leaving the final associations and connections to be made by the clinician. Some may be overly quick to cry resistance where they should cry countertransference (which is harder to cry). Liking and disliking should not really affect the view from the desk, sink or playroom—they can be noted with interest and without the interposition of distorting emotion. The appearance of strong feelings is often less easily identified, and is commonly masked, denied or displaced. These feelings have to be considered as part of the phenomenon of countertransference.

Unrealistic goals are apt to interfere with planning; they would appear to be the most rudimentary kind of misconception on the part of the clinician. He must be wary of the distortion inherent in undue feelings of self-satisfaction, which are likely to arise where narcissistic contemplation of the therapeutic self is substituted for a real treatment plan. Any single planner can be helped by the sensible reminder that it is impossible to substitute a part for the whole; for clinicians, as for others, there is a healthy balance between dependence and independence.

PROFESSIONAL HELPERS

In the course of planning for patients, misconceptions may all too readily arise between professional co-workers. Their number is legion and they may go back to various tribal prejudices, with positive as well as negative expectations. Misconceptions may involve expectations on the basis of race, color and even creed, taking the form of stereotyped ideas of what the Jewish social worker, black street worker, or psychoanalyst can accomplish. Similarly, they may involve the totems of various disciplines in different settings.

Psychiatric nurses have been known to expect doctors to heal the sick; social workers are impatient of doctors' acceptance of the discomfort of physical illness and see this as cold, "scientific" and unfeeling; psychiatrists may actually expect a psychologist to evaluate intellectual capacity. Recent shifts in roles and areas of overlapping responsibility have increased the number of misconceptions which have to be modified by interdependence and mutual respect. Necessary misconceptions probably arise around clinicians as leaders in any setting. They are seen as omnipotent or impotent, capricious or wise, too involved in minutiae or too far removed from detail.

During treatment plannings and at times despite team effort, some of these misconceptions interfere with therapeutic effectiveness by leading to contradiction, ambivalence, and failure of staff to support one another. The need here is for the same kind of communication discussed earlier. The members of all groups, professional and paraprofessional, must understand the other's roles if misconceptions are to be avoided. If their roles are not evaluated and accepted, each by all and all by each, they are not free to turn to planning together for others.

STEREOTYPES OF TREATMENT

In the following units and dyads we are considering some of the stereotypes of treatment which most frequently come up for discussion.

1. THE TEAM APPROACH IS THE MOST COMPREHENSIVE AND THEREFORE THE BEST WAY TO EVALUATE THE PATIENT AND FAMILY.
2. TREATMENT PLANNING IS MOST EFFECTIVE WHEN ALL MEMBERS OF THE TEAM SIT DOWN TOGETHER TO EXPRESS THE POINT OF VIEW REPRESENTED BY THEIR RESPECTIVE DISCIPLINES AND EXPERIENCES.

Let us first question the validity of some aspects of the classical child guidance team—the Holy Trinity, or Royal Family. Once upon a time the King unquestionably assumed his authority as leader. It had been granted him with pomp and circumstance, his title was of the highest rank, and his authority was, at least overtly, recognized by all the subjects of the realm. The Queen assumed the more passive and gentle role, did not publicly question the authority of the King (although she may have given him hell in private and, indeed, sometimes ran the kingdom behind the scenes); her forebears had set a tradition for her as the doer of good works and the Lady Bountiful. The Crown Prince, discontented in his role, had been assigned specific duties. They were his by tradition but he felt that by birth and training he was as good as the King and that his assigned duties, although not transferable, were less prestigious and awesome than the kingly functions. He was sometimes allowed to be openly rebellious, so long as he did not step too far out of line or attempt to replace the King. There were problems for this kingdom.

In the medical setting, the psychiatrist is expected to be the leader of the team, although he may have no particular talent, training or liking for administrative duties or for leadership. Indeed, many of the functions he is expected to perform might be better performed by a member of some other professional discipline, allowing him more time (and very expensive time) to do the thing for which he is best suited—namely, the understanding and treatment of illness and relief of pain. In favor of his position as leader, however, is the fact that his voice carries more authority in the community, and at moments of crisis he continues to be looked to by other disciplines.

The psychologist is the only member of the team who is uniquely trained to perform a function often found essential in arriving at a diagnostic formulation: namely, the administration of psychological tests. Too often, he feels that this function is not putting his talents to their best use—he would like to involve himself much more in "therapy." Perhaps this feeling originates from his failure to receive referrals for whom psychological testing is crucial and without which a diagnostic formulation cannot be made.

If psychological testing is a routine part of every evaluation, it is being overused. It is intesting that psychological testing is much more likely to be routine in child guidance clinic settings, which are "charitable" agencies, and much less frequently needed in the private practice of child psychiatry, where presumably people get the best care of all because they pay so much for it. The question arises: Shouldn't the private psychiatrist use them more (but doesn't in order to save the patient's money), and the public agencies use them less (because they aren't really necessary in certain cases)? The argument is not whether they add an extra dimension to the evaluation, but whether it is a necessary dimension. The psychologist, of course, is frequently trained in and well qualified to do therapy, but no one else is prepared to perform standard psychological testing. Here he is unique.

The social worker, it is assumed, will work with the parents while the child psychiatrist treats the child. Since the family brings the child to the clinic, it is also assumed that the child is the "primary patient" and therefore he is the one who needs "treatment." The parents are regarded as in need of "counseling" to help them understand the child's problems and to modify their reactions to him. Should it be decided and mutually agreed by the psychiatrist and the social worker that either or both parents represent the more serious psychopathology and that the child is reacting to the parents' actions, should not the parents become the primary patients and the child be counseled in how to modify his reactions to the parents? Would the psychiatrist and social worker then change roles? Would they change titles? Would they exchange patients for clients? In most cases, the responsibility for beginning the cycle of action and reaction, or at least the responsibility for changing it, must be laid at the door of the parents as responsible adults.

In brief, team approach in child guidance needs rethinking. Is it really necessary to have the complete background and history of both parents in order to understand the problems of the child? Is it not possible that the child's therapist might better understand the interaction between the child and the parents and the contribution of the parents to the child's problems by having an interview with the parents? In that way, he could talk with them about their child and themselves, rather than listen to someone else's extensive appraisal. If one process could be as useful as the other, the former is certainly far more conserving of professional time than the latter. Is it worth the extensive (expensive) use of professional time during which three or five or seven professionals sit through a two-hour conference to listen to reports and discuss a patient some of them may not have seen or may not see in the future?

3.   PLAY IS FOR CHILDREN, TALKING IS FOR ADULTS.

While play is the natural means of expression for children, many children are able to verbalize feelings in a direct though unsophisticated way, and they should be encouraged to do so. Some 10-year-olds are insulted when introduced to a playroom. Some 14-year-olds are uncomfortable sitting in an office without something to do with their hands. This is not to minimize the value of metaphoric expression for children. While "talking therapy" may deteriorate to visiting at times, it is probably more often the case that "play therapy" becomes simply play, albeit in the service of developing a relationship.

4.   THE GENDER OF THE THERAPIST IS ALL-IMPORTANT TO TREAT-
       MENT PLANNING.

Occasionally, probably rarely, whether the assigned therapist is male or female may make a vital difference in reaching the goals set for the patient. Usually, the patient's response will be based on his problems and on the personality of the therapist. The problems may come out in a different order, but eventually they are likely to appear in any case. It helps for the therapist to have been well-trained and experienced.

5. THE ONLY GOOD THERAPY IS PSYCHOTHERAPY.

There are many equally good treatment plans. The choice among them will depend on the availability of therapy time, the individual differences among therapists, and the particular needs of the patient. Perhaps it is time to stop arguing about good or bad methods and schools of thought in favor of planning treatment selectively based on what is indicated for a certain patient.

6. REGRESSION IN THE COURSE OF THERAPY IS BAD.
   REGRESSION IN THE COURSE OF THERAPY IS GOOD.

In treatment planning regression should at times be expected and encouraged in therapy on the premise that the patient must relive and again work through earlier trauma. Along with this process the parents' understanding should be carefully sought lest they become disturbed and demoralized. A child must never be regarded as a static entity. We must focus on the timing of his push toward growth and give recognition to the great changes that occur in his development and personality from month to month in at least some if not all areas.

7. RAPID SYMPTOM REMOVAL IS BAD.

It is not. It alleviates problems and pain and saves time and expense. It is true that on occasion it does not allow us to get at the cause of the symptom, and the cause will then find another outlet. We suspect that most therapists, particularly tired ones, secretly pat themselves on the back when they successfully remove the symptom. Families don't really mind, either.

8. TRANQUILIZERS ARE VERY USEFUL IN TREATING CHILDREN.
   TRANQUILIZERS ARE OF NO USE IN TREATING CHILDREN.

It is not easy to explain the fact that some sincere, well-trained, objective therapists can find various tranquilizers very useful and effective, while other therapists equally sincere etc. find them of little or no use. The difference must be found in the therapist, his skill in the use of drugs, and perhaps the particular range of patients seen—the greater the overt anxiety, the "better" the response to tranquilizers.

9. SOME CHILDREN ARE UNTREATABLE.

We are reluctant to undertake treatment of children with whom we find it difficult to identify (delinquent, brain-damaged, mentally retarded, socially disadvantaged), or who point up our inability to be flexible and experimental. One supervisor commented that she had heard many therapists complain that they could not relate to a lower-class child, but she had never heard one complain that he could not relate to an upper-class child. Is is even possible to decide not to treat before trying?

10. ALL CHILDREN ARE TREATABLE.

Ask any therapist.

11. POOR AND DEPRIVED CHILDREN HAVE NO LANGUAGE AND LITTLE FANTASY LIFE. THEY CANNOT UNDERSTAND US.

Their speech and its content are different from those of middle-class therapists because communicative skills depend on early stimulation and common referents. Their language is highly expressive. Our inability to understand their fantasy life makes it no less rich. Some things about us they understand too well, and it is we who are defensively reluctant to understand them. Their need for food and housing is not antithetical to psychodynamics or depression.

12. IF WE JUST HAD ENOUGH FOSTER HOMES AND GOOD FOSTER PARENTS WE WOULDN'T NEED INSTITUTIONS FOR CHILDREN.

Because of their early life experiences, some children are unable to relate to and tolerate the intimacy of family living.

In an institutional setting, however, they are able to learn to modify their behavior from an asocial or antisocial direction.

13. MANIPULATION OF PATIENTS OR FAMILIES IS BAD.

Manipulation is bad if it is for the aggrandizement or convenience of the planner. It is not bad if it eases the family stress, affords the experience of improved interpersonal relationships within the family, and allows growth and developmental processes to move ahead in the child. Much of modern therapeutic management requires imaginative and skillful manipulation.

14. IF WE RAISED THE AGE OF MANDATORY SCHOOL ATTENDANCE, WE WOULD KEEP DELINQUENT CHILDREN OFF THE STREETS AND OUT OF TROUBLE.

This would lead to more riots in the schools. It is better to look more carefully at early school experiences. We are likely to find that they fail to stimulate a child's natural curiosity to learn, fail to satisfy his need for self-esteem, fail to channel his urge to compete, and fail to capitalize on those abilities and interests he does develop even though they may not lead him to fulfill the requirements for college admission.

10

THE VICISSITUDES OF TREATMENT PLANNING

THE PRESSURE OF CRISIS AND MULTIPROBLEM CIRCUMSTANCES

Differential treatment planning has been discussed as a complex process involving small groups, conscious decisions, and unconscious motivation in the evolution of a master plan that is understood and accepted by planner and family. There are variations on this theme, plans for in and out, plans for this and that, and alternate plans for optimal plans. In all of this planning the pitch is low, the murmur intellectual, feeling is naturally acceptable but controlled. In fact, there is an admirable hush.

There is another kind of planning which is done in emergency, with urgency. Here the demand for action takes precedence, the plan involves action and, however various the undertones, the overtones are loud and clear. The plan is sometimes made, as noted by the medical student, on the spur of the moment in the middle of the night.

The relationship between this latter kind of treatment planning and that based on the exchange of more complete information in a more formal manner should be kept in mind. A plan is being evolved but in sequence; it is evident from the beginning that planning will take place in steps. It is not hard to decide what takes precedence in the face of assaultive behavior, suicidal attempts, and acute anxiety. The treatment plan answers the immediate need. Hopefully, the first step is taken as the beginning of a continuing plan and not as an end in itself. The ability to move on, with patient and family, to another step may reflect the skill of the planner. Action is not substituted for thought; the connection has to be made between thought and action, but the process is an accelerated one and a difference is made between practical short-term goals and longer-term planning.

It is probable that emergency planning represents a debased form of planning. The tendency is toward action, action within a closed system not offering many alternatives to planner, family or patient. Thus it is an accelerated planning process, and the nature of the plan is determined in large part by the nature of the immediate situation. A number of planners may be involved; their skills lie in an instant recognition of the bare bones of the situation so that their actions will be appropriate.

Psychiatric emergencies arise in all families. However, they occur most often in the public eye for the disorganized poor, who move through life in a series of thumps and bumps, who gravitate without feelings of shame to hospital and police station. The recurrent emergency, for one family member or another, interferes with more thoughtful approaches and becomes part of life style for family and for planner. The constant struggle to stabilize the situation takes the place of other planning, and its momentum often carries family and child away from more complete treatment planning.

In contrast, crisis intervention, where the emergency is neatly delineated and is seen positively as "a turning point," has for some time been the happy hunting ground of all good planners. There, with a series of graded reactions to crisis, families are perceived as available, which indeed they may be, and the six visits for therapy are planned with every expectation of success. Since almost every request for help is taken for a crisis of varying intensity, differentiation of crisis intervention from other kinds of treatment planning may not be warranted.

Case A: Recurrent crisis

At the time of the present referral to the *child psychiatry clinic of a municipal hospital,* Denise, at just 15 years of age, was said to be pregnant. The referral was focused on Mrs. D's insistence that Denise have an abortion and on Denise's apparent wish to have the baby. Mrs. D was basing the indications for an abortion on her quarrel with Denise as to who would take care of the baby. In addition, she said she was angry, as Denise had been truant from school and had stayed away from home for two days the month before. Mother and daughter disagreed as to the date of the last menstrual period, and there was considerable interchange between them about Denise's depression and withdrawal, which alternated with her complaints against her mother and her flamboyant description of her depression. Her mother had found "I want a baby" written in her diary, and Denise reported a nightmare in which the baby came to her and said, "Don't kill me, Mommy." Denise denied understanding the dream and said, "It's not my decision," at the same time that she made her disagreement with her mother all too clear. There seemed to be a real problem in terms of the ambivalence inherent in the relationship between mother and child and the complicated dynamics which underlay a long-standing conflict presented at a superficial level.

Denise had first been referred to the Child Psychiatry Clinic at the age of 11 by her mother with the chief complaint that "anything she's told to do, she does the opposite." Denise herself admitted to depression and headaches; she had heard voices suggesting she lie to her mother and possibly hurt her. Her sister Debra, 9 years of age, was already known to the clinic. Denise was preoccupied with Debra, on whom she was quite dependent. An attempt was made to see Denise and her mother regularly, but this was unsuccessful after four or five visits, as there was a diminution in problems as perceived by mother and daughter. Contact between this family and the clinic thereafter remained sporadic.

In the next two years, Denise and her sister were seen twice each, usually after a dramatic telephone call from their mother, and on two occasions, after somewhat excited telephone calls from school. Denise's mood varied radically between depression and self-satisfaction (acting out for and with her mother at school and in sexual areas), and there was some emphasis on the somatic, with complaints of headaches. On one occasion Mrs. D took Denise to another municipal hospital for admission, but this was at a time that Mrs. D had been reported to the Society for Prevention of Cruelty to Children by a neighbor. Two years after Denise was first seen, when she was 13 years old, it was recommended that she attend a *girls' activity group* on a weekly basis, which she did for the next year. At the same time, she was referred to a *family planning clinic,* as Denise and her mother were both referring to the possibility of pregnancy.

There was serious concern for the effect of a pregnancy on Denise. In spite of, rather than because of, the flamboyance of family style, Denise was thought to be at borderline in personality function and had to be considered as quite fragile. However, she was somewhat immobilized by depression and had withdrawn; it was felt important to encourage her to take an active part in deciding on abortion. It was recommended that Denise be admitted to an obstetrical ward that day but that the decision about abortion be postponed over the weekend.

Denise's *admission to the hospital,* with attendant family approval, allowed her to go along in a healthier fashion with her mother's plan for abortion, although she had little insight into the dynamics of her ambivalence about her pregnancy. The attempt to gain a little more time to reestablish previous ego strengths was unsuccessful, and the surgical procedure was only postponed by chance. Denise had eaten breakfast!

No systematic planning was envisaged for this family in the light of past experience. The clinic continued, with patience and tolerance, to "play it by ear" and make use of whatever therapeutic opportunities future crises would present.

Case B: Multiproblem circumstances

LaVerne, an 11-year-old boy, was referred to *the child psychiatry clinic of a municipal hospital* in the ghetto by his school toward the end of the third grade, which he was repeating. A letter was sent to the mother asking her to call for an appointment. There was no response to this letter, and nothing further was heard until late fall, when the child was again referred by the school.

The first letter from school indicated that LaVerne had had many "learning and behavioral" problems. They felt he was having visual perceptual difficulties and described him as restless and daydreaming, with poor frustration tolerance and increasing loss of control. It was said that he managed to provoke one fight a day and threw objects recklessly when things got out of hand.

The school saw him as a depressed, unhappy child and noted that he had one sister, 18; Mrs. B had mentioned that her husband was an alcoholic who beat LaVerne without provocation. LaVerne had been hospitalized at the age of 6 years for a fracture of a leg after having been hit by a car.

The second letter from the school, 7 months later, referred to hospitalization of LaVerne's mother two months before for surgery and reported that she was being seen daily on an outpatient basis for radiation therapy. Once more, the mother was said to want help for LaVerne, although the emphasis seemed to be on his school behavior.

After several attempts to reach his mother and see LaVerne, the social worker finally met with Mrs. B after one of her appointments at the radiotherapy clinic. There she was given a very poor prognosis and thought to have metastases following cancer of the cervix. Mrs. B was obviously ill and found it difficult to give the details of LaVerne's past history. She had associated coming to get help for LaVerne with possible retardation and was somewhat defensive.

LaVerne and his mother were finally seen by the child psychiatrist after two failed appointments. By this time the school had sent a third anguished letter describing LaVerne as unpredictable, explosive and violent. He had said he wanted to kill himself and that he hoped someone would shoot him. These remarks were reported as having upset his mother, who had beaten him, "although I try not to beat him too much because his stepfather is very hard on LaVerne."

LaVerne was watchful and careful—he was quiet when with his mother but watched her. He warmed up rather quickly during the interview and showed some ability to put his feelings into words. He used a lot of denial and referred quite positively to school. He felt he was "sad" more often than "mad" but agreed that he got mad when he was picked on. He touched on his worries about his mother only tangentially and could not relate this to his troubles at school.

His three wishes were for a minibike, a car, and a pool table. He wanted to be a detective when he got to be 21 and half copied another child's drawing of a cat face with some additional detail.·

LaVerne's mother seemed to be having some difficulty in concentrating but was quick to insist on her role as mother although she was using her daughter Lily, 18 years old, for almost physical support. She said that LaVerne had had no previous illnesses and only one accident. Mrs. B related LaVerne's behavior to failures on the part of schools he had attended, and she was thinking of asking for a transfer. Mrs. B said that LaVerne got upset about her husband but agreed he worried about her—"When I sleep, he whispers to me." In spite of her efforts, Mrs. B was somewhat diffuse, and her functioning was poor enough to raise the question of CNS metastases. (After this interview, during which a plan was made and then acted on, we found that Mrs. B denied all memory of the interview and of the plan.) Mrs. B showed no immediate insight into the serious nature of her illness and fixed her attention on the swelling of her arm, which she said pained her. She agreed that she had been most irregular in her contacts with her radiography clinic but agreed to return to see if they could be of any help.

Treatment plan (LaVerne)

1. LaVerne was to attend a special day school for emotionally disturbed children, and so not spend all day with his sick mother.
2. Concurrently, LaVerne was to see the child psychiatrist at the Clinic on a weekly basis.
3. The social worker was to insure the boy's attendance at school and Clinic.
4. The social worker was also to help Lily get a job, with partial separation from her sick mother. Lily was in considerable need of emotional support, to be obtained through sporadic contact with the social worker.
5. Mrs. B was to be helped to return to the Clinic and also to maintain the most appropriate defenses against threat of illness (social worker).
6. Pressure was to be brought to bear on the stepfather to "go easy" on LaVerne at this difficult time (threat of court order).
7. The family as a whole was to be prepared for the death of mother during this terminal phase.

This plan was practical if imperfect. It was based on an understanding of the reaction of three family members to chronic and undoubtedly fatal illness and their ability to use concrete help. Mrs. B was relieved to find support for herself and acceptance for LaVerne. She allowed him to attend the special school regularly after visiting it herself. Her illness was long drawn out, and although she attended the radiography clinic, it involved continued grieving on the part of both children. LaVerne did not have sufficient psychic energy to maintain individual therapeutic contacts in the Clinic away from the school setting, but was able to form relationships there and learn. Lily tended to withdraw and found it hard to accept suggestions which took her out of the house and into competitive situations. Further treatment planning for LaVerne and Lily had to wait on the final course of their mother's illness.

THE CIRCUMSTANCE OF THE PLANNER

In the exercise in planning that follows, a series of consultants from markedly different clinical settings were invited to construct treatment plans based on their impressions of diagnostic vignettes of two cases. The influence of the setting, the varying theoretical frameworks, different professional styles and, perhaps, different training experiences are well demonstrated. To convey the flavor fully the comments have been left untouched. They were all made "blindly."

Case C: Thanatophobia in an 11-year-old girl

Janie is an 11-year-old girl, the third of five children. Help is sought by the mother because Janie in recent months has become very anxious and fearful of death. She has developed many somatic complaints by which she avoids school but for which the family doctor can find no physical explanation. Her school performance has not suffered and she continues to be an above-average performer in all areas, reasonably well liked by classmates and teachers. She is very helpful to her mother at home with chores and the younger children, but has lately, on occasion, become very rude to her. Relationships with her siblings seem rather typical of a well-integrated large family.

There is nothing in her history that would arouse particular attention except some separation anxiety on starting school and the fact that 9 months earlier the family moved to a different city from the one in which Janie had grown, and to a different house and school district when they purchased a house three months ago.

The mother gives the impression of being a very solid person whose demands of life are fairly modest, who enjoys her family and her role in it. She exudes good common sense, and one is somewhat surprised to learn that she is a strong believer of a very fundamentalist religious dogma. Their religion is a compelling aspect of family life but she has allowed her oldest child to disengage himself from the church, believing that each has to find his own way to salvation. The children appear to have a good deal of freedom and there are no strong currents of overt rebellion or withdrawn passivity in the family.

The father comes through less strongly, not because of passivity so much as his nonverbal quality. He seems to be responsible and quite devoted to his family. One senses that he will generally let his wife take the lead and go along with her decisions but will occasionally put his foot down, at which point she defers to his wishes, probably manipulating things so that everyone is satisfied.

Janie shows some separation anxiety on going to the playroom and the mother genuinely reassures her. She is not interested in playing with toys or games and verbalizes her anxieties quite well. She is unhappy about the move, having liked the old home much better. "Kids are different here." She is angry at her mother but doesn't know why. She feels guilty that her father has to work so hard to support the large family. She is afraid he might get sick. School is OK once she gets there, but she sometimes has "this awful scared feeling" when she wakes up in the morning. She is afraid she will die or that there will be an atomic war and she will go to hell because she hasn't been good enough. She is obviously distressed, occasionally tearful, and sincere. She appears to be in good touch with reality and to demonstrate in many areas the common sense so apparent in her mother. She tries to apply this to the painful areas, but to no avail. She is hopeful that the therapist will be able to get rid of these worries for her.

Suggested treatment plans (Janie)

a) Consultant from a busy ghetto clinic (Impressions). An 11-year-old girl, prepubertal to pubertal, has experienced two recent moves or dislodgments as precipitating factors for the onset of mild but distressing anxiety attacks with phobic manifestations. The dynamics involve the crumbling of the child's previous defenses of denial, sublimation in the face of puberty, and awareness of her own vulnerability—based on the mother's identification with painful goodness and the child's anger, and the father's identification with love and the child's vulnerability to loss. These imbalances are internal and are very unlikely to respond to any "neatening" process from the outside; therefore, the need is to institute the kind of treatment best suited to neurotic disorder, albeit with hope for a fairly rapid resolution if the family is basically as good as it looks. The diagnosis is a phobic neurosis and the following treatment plan is suggested:

An immediate interview with the mother, the father, and Janie by a psychiatrist and a social worker as a therapeutic start. The interview would also allow for an estimate of the family's treatability and of the need to involve two of the staff rather than one. The probable need for treatment would be used as a focus to explore the father's role as hero, the mother's role as villain, Janie's guilt and badness, and evidence of insight into the intellectual understanding of anxiety and somatic components, the nature of the phobic defenses, the possible role of religion, and other factors.

An immediate telephone call to the school, (social worker,

psychiatrist, or psychiatric nurse) warning them not to trade on Janie's goodness, encouraging them to continue making intellectual demands on her, and asking them to make special efforts to involve her in the everyday life of the school. Somatic complaints should be explained to them psychologically.

An immediate conference with the family doctor regarding his role in helping Janie by accepting her negative feelings as related to her age, and by accepting the validity of her physical complaints as they relate to anger, fear and other feelings.

A meeting with the clergy should be avoided unless specifically requested by the mother.

In view of our marked limitations in staff and staff time, and considering the need to respond to an emergency effectively, the case could be continued with the social worker seeing the mother and father, and the psychiatrist seeing Janie. Also in view of the family's apparent ability to function successfully, it would seem sufficient to confine the problem to these three and not involve the entire family, until proved necessary. Treatment would start with half-hour sessions, which can always be wrung out of the week of already overworked staff, and would continue for three to six months.

b) Consultant from a large medical center in a small university town. An initial conjoint family interview should be set up in order to assess directly some of the family communication patterns—for example, the role played by the father in the interaction between mother and patient. Also, further exploration of certain developmental lines might conceivably show some relationship to the presenting picture, like patterns of sibling relationships, sexual development, pubescent status, and so forth.

Thereafter, outpatient individual psychotherapy for Janie, initially twice a week because of her acute disturbance, then once a week, with parents seen periodically for counseling in the management of Janie to maintain open communication and avoid major obstruction. Any major overhaul of the parents' personality structure or interaction of an inter-personal nature is unlikely. The initial phase of therapy should be primarily oriented toward symptomatic relief, with environmental emphasis on return to school very early if not immediately. Here it is likely that work with parents and school authorities would be needed to some extent, although probably minimal resistance is to be anticipated in accomplishing this early objective.

Psychotherapeutic goals (approach by short-term therapy of three months or less): Initial efforts with Janie would center on establishing a therapeutic relationship in the expectation of moving fairly early into her overt concern with anger at her mother, the sense of loss with the family move, conflicts stirred up by puberty, and the need to get her back into the mainstream of early adolescent development.

Note. In a medical center this case might very well be handled by a child psychiatry resident with supervision from the senior staff. If there were a waiting list, this case would be taken into treatment immediately on the general principle that school phobias are considered urgent if not emergency cases. While it is possible that a social worker could be assigned to the case to work with the parents, it would be preferable for one person to manage the total case. The prognosis is good.

c) Consultant from a psychoanalytically oriented clinic in a large town. Janie, an obsessional girl in early puberty, reacts to the loss of her peers and her familiar home and school environment with neurotic symptoms. She defends against feelings of sadness, anger and anxiety by developing phobias, conversion symptoms and a fear of death. She suffers from a reactive disorder which warrants quick and appropriate short-term intervention centered on the theme of feelings aroused by loss and change. At the same time, the parents need help in understanding what is going on in their daughter and encouragement in facilitating Janie's adjustment. They can help her develop a new circle of friends and through their understanding reassure the girl by helping her venture out rather than retreat. This could be accomplished by work with parents and child on the part of the same person or through the collaborative efforts of two workers (as long as they pursue a similar course). Choice of one or two would depend on the preference of Janie and her parents, the skills and working comfort of the therapist(s), and other practical matters. The family could be seen together (family therapy) or Janie and the parents separately. The case lends itself to a variety of options. Only contact with the live person can determine the best approach.

However, the feeling about and adjustments to loss and change should be the leitmotiv for the treatment of the family, since I suspect that Janie is not only reacting to her own feelings but those of the rest of the family as well. It seems important to first address oneself to the ongoing crisis by a time-limited approach.

Even if more chronic difficulties come out into the open after seeing the child and family for a diagnostic "first," I would still suggest short-term intervention strictly around the recent loss and in the context of change (developmental and temporal), leaving the door open for the possibility that Janie may want to return for more intensive long-term treatment at a later time.

Her symptoms make it clear that this is an obsessional girl who may run into trouble during adolescence if sexual impulses have to be strongly defended against and if the attachment to her mother would turn out to be more ambivalent and interfere with her ability to emancipate herself from the family orbit.

d) Consultant from a busy private practice in a large city.
A "soft" school phobia, or anxiety state, characterized by somatic complaints and fears in a late latency or prepubescent girl whose adaptive behavior was seemingly adequate until two family moves within the past year precipitated separation anxiety and accentuated dependency needs.

Although we don't know the age spread or sex of the sibs or her relationship with the older sibs, I would wonder about the level of sophistication and range of physical development of her new schoolmates and what they talk about—which may have contributed to a breakdown of her defenses. It is quite possible that her symptoms would have appeared even without the moves because they are so pubescent in nature.

I agree with Janie that she needs some psychotherapeutic help about which I would talk with her and her parents. Some psychiatrists would possibly do family therapy, or refer them for this. I would feel that her personal crisis is such that she should have individual therapy. I would see parents as necessary for a while until I got more clues from Janie as to their roles and depending partly on the sexual content of her concerns, partly on her fears of growing up.

I would not know until later on in therapy whether the symptoms represent a maturational crisis or whether there are more deeply pervasive difficulties.

I would hold in abeyance plans to enrich her social life, such as extracurricular activities the school or the church might arrange until Janie helps throw more light on her own reactions. By the same token I would not think of consulting the minister of a fundamentalist church unless I knew him or her.

With the close family ties, I would explore Janie's urges to move away from the family a little, as well as her parents' understanding of her need to do so, which is promising in light of their letting the older boy move away from the church. However, the role of church tenets and conscience in patient and family would need to be assessed and utilized in view of what appears to be a stirring away from compliance toward individuation on the part of the patient.

e) Consultant from a state mental health clinic in a large city. Time-limited therapy for Janie (three to five months), with a focus on unresolved feelings about separation from and loss of female objects—including mother herself (symbolically "lost" once more as Janie grows into adolescence) and her prepuberty chum, presumably lost when the family moved.

The caseworker should set up periodic discussions with the parents, together, to help them understand Janie's problem, verbalize their own feelings about the move, and give permission for all family members to express their feelings about the family dislocation.

Note.—This case falls far to the healthy end of the spectrum of families seen at our child guidance clinic. Multiproblem fatherless families are much more typical.

f) Consultant in private practice in a small town. I would explain to the mother that Janie has many strengths, such as her school performance, her good relationships with people both in and outside the family, her helpfulness and concern about others, and her realistic and mature judgment about most things. I would point to the plight of the middle child, who frequently gets lost in a large family. Encourage the mother to be patient with Janie's occasional rudeness, which appears to be a manifestation both of a healthy effort to need her mother less and of the anxiety she is temporarily experiencing. Be certain the mother understands that Janie's fears are acutely experienced and are not manipulation. Explain to the mother how Janie's preoccupation with death probably leads to the somatic complaints which are, of course, very real to Janie. She hurts, but they also bring security in keeping her close to mother and home. The two rapid moves suggest that this is partly situational. I would further explore with the mother Janie's sexual history and question whether menarche might be involved with the somatic complaints.

I would further explore the family religious beliefs for what they may have conveyed to Janie about good and evil and her responsibility. This would probably lead to the suggestion that her mother deemphasize religion to Janie for a while, especially the frightening aspects (damnation, hell fire, approaching judgment). When she does have to bring religious beliefs into focus for Janie, she should concentrate on the loving, forgiving, Good Father aspects of their beliefs. I would ask the mother's permission to explore with Janie her religious fears, her preoccupations with death, her fears about her own lack of goodness, with mother knowing full well that I don't share her religious beliefs and might question some of them with Janie. I would impress the mother with the importance of insisting that Janie go to school, in the hope of preventing the development of a full-blown school phobia.

I would recommend psychotherapy with Janie and want to see her twice a week on the basis that she is acutely anxious and it is important to establish a trusting relationship quickly. After a few weeks, the frequency of appointments can probably be reduced. The mother should be available so that we can occasionally take a part of Janie's session and talk together to validate what Janie has told me and to counsel the mother on her reactions to Janie. I would reassure the mother that their relationship seems basically stable and healthy and acknowledge her good capacity for wise mothering.

Psychotherapy would begin by reassuring Janie that I understand the pain she is suffering, that it is important to continue school, and that she needs her relationships with other people even though it is often very hard to work at them. I hope and expect to be able to help her with these problems, which we will explore together. Acknowledging her strong points, such as her verbal ability, I would explain that during our sessions either playing or talking is acceptable and useful. I would discuss the connection between anxiety and somatic symptoms and begin to explore the occasions and sources of her acute discomfort. Tranquilizers would not be recommended in the early stage of treatment. While they might make Janie more comfortable, the comfort would interfere with her motivation for talking things out. If she does not show fairly rapid improvement (a few weeks of treatment), I would probably recommend the use of tranquilizers along with psychotherapy.

Case D: Disruptive classroom behavior in an 8-year-old boy

Billy is an 8-year-old boy, the older of two children, referred by the school because of disruptive behavior in the classroom. He "has to be on the go all the time," attracts attention through subtle provocative interactions with other students, and procrastinates about his teacher's demands. Grades are low but passing—potential is felt to be much higher. On the playground he usually avoids or is ignored by the other boys, sometimes staying by himself and sometimes playing around the girls.

At home Billy has frequent tantrums. He is very jealous of a four-year-old brother whom he openly states is favored. He seems to disobey direct orders of parents deliberately as if to show his independence, but when defending himself he claims to have forgotten or misunderstood. Frequently he wanders off and is gone for hours from home in defiance of his parents' instructions. He is reluctant to go to bed at night and is frequently enuretic. Otherwise, his sleeping, eating and eliminative habits are appropriate.

Pregnancy, birth, developmental and health histories are unremarkable. The mother is a passive, mildly depressed, mousy woman who is overwhelmed by his behavior and her inability to handle it. She weeps easily as she talks. She fears the younger child is beginning to copy Billy's behavior. The father, a stern disciplinarian and a perfectionist in his demands on himself and his family, is alternately angry and amused as he reports his son's misadventures. He works long hours and spends little time with his children. When he does, it is strictly on his terms and Billy usually "blows it."

In the playroom Billy is spontaneous, curious and aggressive, but is easily controlled by verbal requests and responsive to suggestions. There is no separation anxiety. He wants the therapist included in his play and chooses toys that allow expression of aggression and competition. He soon loses interest in an activity if he can't master it quickly or senses he will lose in competition. He is overly cheerful and not overtly anxious, but one senses a sadness and an inability to relax. He volunteers information about experiences in which he plays a brave or heroic role with little concern for credibility. He will talk about his family when a question is asked but otherwise avoids it. He asks about other children in the playroom and is reluctant to leave at conclusion of the session, requiring slight physical coaxing toward the door.

Suggested treatment plans (Billy)

a) Consultant from a busy ghetto clinic. Billy is an 8-year-old boy who has opted, of necessity, for symptoms rather than for actual development of his own personality. He displaces anxiety over nonbeing (which mirrors parents) to sib and displaces anger to school. Rewards are from the father's and mother's reactions to his misbehavior. Billy is attempting to relieve his own discomfort through regression, through direct expression of anger, and by a gradual reduction of the need to feel. This is a behavor disorder of childhood, avoidance type.

Absence from home for "several hours" must be considered serious unless the family does not see it as a problem—"he was around," "I knew he was there." Actually, in a ghetto setting he would tend to respond with excitement calculated to encourage the family to become excited (I suspect this is a middle-class overstatement!).

Treat this as a chronic problem with a relatively poor prognosis in view of the description of a mousy mother and a perfectionistic father who show no indication of mutual pleasure in family life.

A conference should be set up with mother, father and Billy to discuss the presenting problem and Billy's tendency to disappear in a number of different situations. Make specific suggestions about further evolution of pride and pleasure, using some positive feature which *must* have been left out of history. Raise the question of seeing the mother and father separately and/or together every two weeks or once a month and be clear as to the probable relationship of their problems to Billy's view of his family, himself and his school (in that order).

I suggest a supervised after-school program (daily activity group) for Billy. Start with the staff's insight into Billy's fear of committing himself, the self-destructive nature of his anger, which has been whittled down to size. Look for a successful experience in this setting as a basis for improvement in school and a more positive approach from the parents in reaction to his success in some area.

Provide tutoring under supervision of the clinic. School failure is secondary to inattention and disruptive behavior, which could be corrected up to a point with remedial help.

A conference with the school (by letter or telephone) would absorb anger and frustration and divert these feelings from Billy. I would interpret the limitations of psychiatric help where the family is limited in its ability to change, without completely disrupting any comforting notions members may have of themselves and one another. I would acknowledge the frustrations of dealing with a child who "will not learn" and is disruptive, and I would offer a description of the treatment plan.

Review the treatment plan after three months and evaluate progress before working out any plan for further treatment.

The plan would then start off in low key for the parents, twice weekly or monthly, with follow-up visits for Billy and mother. Daily after-school program and weekly tutoring sessions for the boy. Following this first stage, and built upon it, the next stage would be planned. One needs to consider this case in stages.

b) Consultant from a large medical center in a small university town. Visit the school to observe the patterns of Billy's behavior related to anxiety and conflict arousal. Also, begin a relationship with the teacher, whose assistance in his management will be crucial in promoting "corrective emotional experiences" with regard to competition, success, achievement and sharing—*at the appropriate time during the therapy.*

I would recommend psychological testing, and perhaps a general physical examination, to assess intellectual potential or the possibility of "soft" neurological issues (unlikely).

Set up one conjoint family session to observe their interactions as grist for the therapeutic mill—for example, the boy's internalized problem as observed in the externalized interaction with the father. (One of my staff indicates that in this case he would invite himself to dinner in the family home or by some other means intrude himself into the family interaction on its own home ground. Given the opportunity, perhaps after the child patient went to bed, he would then chat with both spouses and attempt to elicit a bit of past history concerning each of them in the presence of the other.)

This case raises the question of individual versus family therapy. Certainly a case might be made for either approach, with some opinion probably oriented toward individual therapy for Billy because of the signals in his diagnostic interview regarding his needs, and in view of his ability to relate and respond positively to an interested person. This suggests that a relationship could be established rather readily as a solid base for dealing with later transference problems when he becomes more aggressive and starts testing limits. This school of thought would likely have the parents seen in partial therapy, perhaps by a social worker in a collaborative venture. Others would suggest seeing the family together (mother, father, Billy, and perhaps occasionally the younger sibling, too) to emphasize the "playing out" in their interaction of the interpersonal conflicts that express Billy's intrapsychic conflicts, with the objectives of modifying interactions, helping the mother to become more adequate, the father more warm, giving and consistent. I would be inclined to consider it almost impossible to help Billy without changing the parents and thus might proceed by alternating individual and family sessions for a total of two sessions each week. I expect outpatient therapy would require approximately a year, and would be done by a child psychiatry resident who would keep in close touch with the schoolteacher, maintaining her as a therapeutic team member, giving her management suggestions and expecting her to become more attuned to reporting differential behavior patterns. Medication, although a possibility, might then be easier to do without. A day treatment program might be used for a more intensive treatment approach if progress is slow or if more serious problems became evident in the school visit.

c) Consultant from a busy private practice in a large city. Billy is somewhat depressed due to unresolved problems from the oedipal state, sibling rivalry, and unsatisfactory parental relationships which do not give support to his need for encouragement and success. The father is strict, unyielding and belittling; the mother a "feather pillow," depressed.

I would find out if the father is modifiable and how he sees Billy. Are there any areas of identification with him? Can he see his son's frustration in trying to live up to him? Or that there might be areas of mutual enjoyment for each. I'd try a few spaced interviews with the father.

Evaluate the degree of the mother's depression to see whether treatment for her is needed or whether the relationship between father and mother needs strengthening (perhaps neither the mother nor Billy has enough of the father with his long hours of hard work). What is her pattern of mothering? Does she infantilize the patient? What are her expectations of him?

Find out from Billy what he sees as problems and what he thinks would help. What assets does he have? It may take two or three interviews—or more—to get some ideas about these issues.

Search for possible sources of satisfaction elsewhere for Billy. I would communicate to the teacher and the school that he is not "bad" but needs success, dignity and respect. Is there anything he does well at school? In the community, is there an after-school program? An organized boys group, competitive but with realistic expectations of unevenness of performance as "normal"—with a man leader—would be ideal. (In private practice, I would have to do all this exploration myself as well as follow up on it.)

d) Consultant from a state mental health clinic in a large city. A time-limited therapy should be provided for Billy with a male therapist (three to five months) which focuses on improving his self-esteem by supporting the successful expression of competitive strivings in age-appropriate ways.

I would make a tentative recommendation to involve Billy in a latency boys' activity group program (not necessarily activity therapy) in the community during the termination phase of his brief therapy.

There should be time-limited casework with Billy's mother that focuses on resolving her guilt about setting appropriate limits for Billy and that would encourage her to respect her own emotional needs. I would tentatively recommend group therapy in a mothers' group following termination of time-limited casework, if further help seems needed.

Billy's therapist should meet with his father on the father's terms to help him appreciate his own importance to Billy and meet Billy's legitimate needs in the father-son relationship more effectively. The therapist should remain a consultant to father and son after termination of brief therapy.

If individual short-term services were unavailable, activity group therapy for Billy and mothers' group therapy for his mother would be an alternative plan. The male activity group leader would perform the role outlined for the father.

e) Consultant in private practice in a small town. With the parents, I would first point out Billy's strengths: He has no apparent organic complications or intellectual deficits, he reaches out to make closer relationships, evinces curiosity and interest in the world, shows responsiveness to requests, and maintains control in a situation where the adult can give Billy his sole attention. Then I would share their worry about some aspects of their son's ability to get along with people and to learn to grow. Billy is quite immature. Much of his behavior is more appropriate for a 5-year-old; but at times he acts like a much older and more independent child. He's not satisfied to be an 8-year-old and so can find little satisfaction at any of the three levels. He demands the center of attention, he wants to excel, and he seeks admiration through telling heroic but incredible stories. He is unwilling to compete in a situation unless he is sure to win. He has little self-confidence and a poor self-image—he doesn't like himself very much. His high level of anxiety keeps him moving constantly and he hasn't learned to tolerate frustration. One of the things that may confuse Billy is the inconsistency between the ways his mother and his father approach him. Father comes on very strong in his demands and Billy doesn't think he can perform well enough to satisfy Father. Mother approaches so passively that Billy doesn't think he has to meet her demands. He is confused by father's alternation between anger and amusement over his delinquencies. Therefore, he has to test the limits constantly to find out what's really expected of him.

The parents need to agree between themselves what demands are really important and jointly enforce them, and then ignore lots of annoying little things that really aren't important in the long run. They need to praise him for reasonable satisfaction of expectations both at home and at school. Billy needs some time alone, apart from his brother, with each of his parents, but especially with his father. Father must find some activities he can enjoy with Billy. Small tasks and rewards will convey the idea that there are both privileges and responsibilities to being the older child.

I would impress them with Billy's need for greater interaction and success with boys his age. A well-supervised boys' club program would provide play activities with other boys and expose him to controlled doses of competitive and aggressive play. He would achieve some success, increase his "boy" skills, and learn to tolerate frustration and failure once in a while as he learns that at other times he will achieve success. Or as an alternative, a mature high-school boy might be hired as a tutor-companion for Billy to devote some hours each week to play activities with Billy toward the same goals.

I would recommend that we try Billy on a mild tranquilizer, which might help him to slow down somewhat in his activities and increase his attention span and frustration tolerance (it is also sometimes helpful in controlling enuresis).

I would ask the parents' permission to talk with Billy's teacher, both to understand better how she sees his behavior in the classroom, and to offer her some suggestions as to how she might be more helpful to Billy. I would want the teacher to know that he is on medication so that she would note any changes in his behavior, and I would ask her to keep me informed.

Psychological testing would be helpful but not crucial in further ruling out a hyperkinetic syndrome and in establishing his intellectual level so as to keep the parents' and teacher's expectations of him in line with his abilities; also it might inform us further about Billy's perception of his family and his role in the family.

I would further recommend play therapy with Billy, since Billy is reaching out for a relationship of acceptance and respect. Through the metaphor of play he will be able to express, understand and cope better with some of the problems he is unable to verbalize. Concurrently, I would spend time with the parents to help them realize their reactions to Billy and his disruptiveness. Help the mother find ways by which she can cope with Billy's behavior, resume her role as a mother, and find pleasure in Billy and in her relationship with him. Encourage the father to become less demanding of Billy, to find ways to relax with the boy, and to understand his ambivalence about his son's behavior.

I would then talk with Billy, and in simpler terms relate much of what I had said to his parents and how I thought I could be of help to him.

SUMMARY AND CONCLUSION

It would seem from the presentation of these vignettes, and as has been maintained throughout this book, that treatment planning is a function of a number of complex variables, among them the nature of the disorder, the age, sex, and social class of the child, the family pathology, the cooperation of the parents, the geographical location, and, most crucial, the experience and outlook of the practitioner. Despite these many influences, it is surprising how much the recommendations of various practitioners reveal they have in common and how similarly the cases are viewed by them in terms of diagnosis and prognosis. Janie, with her largely internalized disorder at a period of crisis, is given a short-term psychotherapy plan by most of the clinicians; while Billy, with his largely externalized disorder, obtains a prescription of family therapy and treatment in an activity group. What appears to vary is the extent of the dynamic formulation, the range of environmental manipulation, and the differing sense of urgency felt by the different clinicians from different settings.

This report on treatment planning stems from the collective experience and thinking of a group of child psychiatrists trained at different institutions and presently working in a wide variety of clinical settings. Nevertheless, they share an approach to the child and his environment that is developmental, dynamic, holistic and representative of child psychiatric practice in this country today.

Although it covers ground that has received scant attention in the literature, any claim this report may have to advancing psychiatric knowledge and technique lies less in content than in the fact that it collates many different aspects of the topic into a comprehensive, unified, illustrated, and logically developed framework calculated to be of particular advantage in training and teaching.

In this book, planning is seen as a psychosocial process carried out by people, with people, and for people in a co-operative venture. As such, one would expect the progress of the venture to be punctuated by interactional pitfalls and this proved to be the case, as indicated in the text. Like every act of human cooperation, the begetting of trust and confidence was shown to be crucial to the maintenance of continuity in planning.

STATEMENT OF PURPOSE

THE GROUP FOR THE ADVANCEMENT OF PSYCHIATRY has a membership of approximately 300 psychiatrists, most of whom are organized in the form of a number of working committees. These committees direct their efforts toward the study of various aspects of psychiatry and the application of this knowledge to the fields of mental health and human relations.

Collaboration with specialists in other disciplines has been and is one of GAP's working principles. Since the formation of GAP in 1946 its members have worked closely with such other specialists as anthropologists, biologists, economists, statisticians, educators, lawyers, nurses, psychologists, sociologists, social workers, and experts in mass communication, philosophy, and semantics. GAP envisages a continuing program of work according to the following aims:

1. To collect and appraise significant data in the field of psychiatry, mental health, and human relations;
2. To reevaluate old concepts and to develop and test new ones;
3. To apply the knowledge thus obtained for the promotion of mental health and good human relations.

GAP is an independent group, and its reports represent the composite findings and opinions of its members only, guided by its many consultants.

COMMITTEE ACKNOWLEDGMENTS

The Committee on Child Psychiatry prepared this report under the chairmanship of E. James Anthony, M.D. The Committee also wishes to acknowledge the assistance of Suzanne T. van Amerongen, M.D., and William S. Langford, M.D., in the formulation of the report and of Ginsburg Fellows Percy D. Mitchell, M.D., Stephen Proskauer, M.D., and Peter Whitis, M.D.